Women's Work

Home-Style Hoodoo Spells
for
Marriage, Sex, and Motherhood

by Aura Laforest

Lucky Mojo Curio Company
Forestville, California

⇝ 2017 ⇜

Women's Work:
Home-Style Hoodoo Spells for Marriage, Sex, and Motherhood
by Aura Laforest

Text:
Aura Laforest, catherine yronwode

Editor:
catherine yronwode

Cover:
Greywolf Townsend, Unknown Artist

Art:
Charles C. Dawson, R.C. Adams, K. Rudin,
Three Unknown Artists, Greywolf Townsend

Typesetter:
catherine yronwode

Production:
nagasiva yronwode, catherine yronwode

Selections from the following previously published materials are used by permission:
"Hoodoo in Theory and Practice" by catherine yronwode at
LuckyMojo.com/hoodoo.html © 1994-2017 catherine yronwode. "The Lucky
Mojo Free Spells Archive" at LuckyMojo.com/spells.html © 1994-2017 catherine
yronwode. Lucky Mojo Curio Company Forum at Forum.LuckyMojo.com
© 2008-2017 The Lucky Mojo Curio Company

First Edition 2017

Published by
The Lucky Mojo Curio Company
6632 Covey Road
Forestville, California 95436
LuckyMojo.com

ISBN: 978-0-9961471-4-9

Printed in Canada.

TABLE OF CONTENTS

ⅅEDICATION

This book is dedicated to the Spirit and Souls of the African-American people who made the work, and to whom it intrinsically belongs.

Thank you for allowing me to visit your rich and fascinating tradition and please permit me to humbly convey some of its wisdom and practical use to others.

⅋CKNOWLEDGEMENTS

This volume would never have been possible without the encouragement and support of catherine and nagasiva yronwode. Their patience and technical help ensured the fruition of the project. Meanwhile, the computer and software support of both nagasiva and Professor Porterfield made the page layout and editing process possible.

In case you don't know it, any good book is the product of a really great editor – and Miss cat is one of the best I've had the pleasure of working with. In fact, if it hadn't been for Miss cat, I probably never would have started writing at all. As a result, may I always remember to send her chocolate!

Special thanks go to ConjureMan Ali, Turnsteel, nagasiva yronwode, catherine yronwode, Madame Nadia, Madame Pamita, Charles Porterfield, Magdalyna, Miss Phoenix, Deacon Millett, Pamela Wells, Khi Armand, Devi Spring, and Miss Aida for sharing their traditional and original spells.

Meanwhile, my Husband and Son have been the rock solid foundation upon which I have rested as this book has come to be. Many of the passages were mused upon and pondered as I suckled the little one. Chapters in progress were read to my Husband for his input and opinion. Together we discussed many of the issues that are tackled in the various sections of the book and his thoughts lace the sentences you read, along with my own.

To my clients, I extend the final words of thanks. It is a privilege to be able to accompany you all on your individual paths. Each and every one of you is a wellspring of inspiration, an example of strength, of human beauty and of infinite potential.

Introduction

African-American folk magic, familiarly known as hoodoo, conjure, or rootwork, is a practice that I've come to love and respect profoundly.

Rootwork traditions teach us metaphysical and spiritual ways to deal with life, from simple situations, such as luck-changing, to complex romantic, legal, and financial crises. Slowly but steadily, and sometimes not so slowly, this common sense way of working has the capacity to effect change in our lives. I've seen it do so in many ways, most significantly when the practice is woven into the multiple facets of daily life.

Conjure practitioners are told not to ignore daily social life and the physical actions required to reach a goal. We soon learn what happens to magic when the mundane is ignored: The seeds planted by the best of spell-work will sprout poorly, and may not find fertile soil in which to grow.

This book therefore is a reconnection of the magical with the mundane. It addresses not only an occult and folkloric approach to a situation using the spell-casting techniques that hoodoo provides, but also looks at the mindsets which generate our predicaments. It provides building blocks to moving from where we are to where we want to be.

In a literal sense, the food we eat can nourish and grow our bodies or it can poison us. Spiritually, all of the endeavours we set our minds to act as food for our souls, and thus all of our thoughts and actions can either help or hinder our lives. This applies to work, to play, and to magic.

As the title makes clear, this book is primarily aimed at women, but much of the advice and information is useful to all who want to improve their condition. While novices to the practice of hoodoo will probably want to start at the beginning and read through to the end, more experienced practitioners can jump directly to the subjects of interest.

Ultimately however, if the suggestions of this volume stay within the pages, they won't do much for you. I therefore encourage you to experiment with the techniques, the spells, and the attitudes, and make them yours. Cast your doubt aside and give the tools presented herein a chance to make a difference in how you live and experience the world around you. Let rootwork accompany you as you negotiate and deal with the challenges life brings. It has changed my life down to the core in a very positive way.

WHY THIS BOOK IS CALLED "WOMEN'S WORK"

Many of the tools, techniques, and spiritual spells covered in this book may seem to suffer from gender-bias. They appear to be based upon the patriarchal stereotype of "women's work" as labour performed in or around the home. Rather than apologize for this, I choose to celebrate the cultural context out of which home-style conjure emerged.

African-American women, from slavery, to freedom, to now, have helped themselves and their families with magic. Household hoodoo has been an intrinsic part of the daily activities in many black homes since the era when such tasks were automatically gender-assigned.

Remember that rootwork existed long before Harriet Tubman, Mary McLeod Bethune, Rosa Parks, Fannie Lou Hamer, and the civil rights struggle, long before Shirley Chisholm, Oprah Winfrey, Michelle Obama, and the broadening of opportunities for black women in society. At one time black women were restricted to jobs as household servants, hair dressers, and cooks — and while carrying out their duties, they developed specific conjure methods to secure greater incomes, better conditions, and more respectful treatment from employers who were often far from ideal.

Even now, when a black woman can be the First Lady of the land, cooking, cleaning, and laundry still occupy a central place in the upkeep of any home, and the adaptivity of housework to rootwork is well understood by black women. Thus, no matter whether household chores are performed in the context of family life or as part of a job or career in professional child-care, nursing, or janitorial work (or by men as well as women), "women's work" can help you with your spouse, family, or employer — to guide them, protect them, ensure their prosperity, rule them, control them, cross them up, or clear out crossed conditions.

Elaborate spell-casting setups and complex incantations can and do have their place in some magical traditions. However, contrary to what films and television shows portray, when it comes to hoodoo, the stuff of daily life is the core of the work, because simple, home-style spells are accessible to every woman, and weaving magic seamlessly into the fiber of everyday life makes its effects long-lasting and continuous. Domestic conjure that is deployed week after week, year after year, generates a magical momentum that increases over time, and can be maintained almost as a habit. "Women's Work" is rootwork, pure and simple.

ᴀ 𝕽ootworking 𝖁ocabulary

Like all specialized subjects, hoodoo has its own terms of art. The list below is not exhaustive, but it does bring together a glossary of the words you will be most likely to encounter in these pages:

Binding: Causing a person to be restrained, or tied. See Tying Nature.

Client: A person who has work done by a hoodoo practitioner.

Condition: A set of circumstances or a situation being changed or improved through the use of hoodoo.

Condition Supplies: See Spiritual Supplies.

Confused in Mind: A state induced by dominating or crossing spell-work which causes mental fogginess, aimlessness, difficulty in concentration or insomnia.

Conjure: See Hoodoo.

Container Spell: A spell worked within a container such as a fabric or leather mojo bag, locket, jar, doll, egg, bowl, box, bottle, aluminum foil, or plant pot. The container can be permanent or temporary.

Crossed Conditions: Negative circumstances affecting a person as a result of someone working roots. These conditions can affect health, mind, sexuality, money, family relationships, work, or luck.

Crossing: The act of intentionally putting crossed conditions on someone through hurtful spell-work. For more on crossing see:

    LuckyMojo.com/crossing.html

Fixing: The act of preparing an item, such as clothing, floor wash, or a candle, for use in a spell; the item is said to be fixed or dressed.

Hoodoo: African-American folk magic, also known as conjure, rootwork, tricking, or working roots. For more on hoodoo see:

    LuckyMojo.com/hoodoohistory.html
    LuckyMojo.com/hoodooandreligion.html

Hoodoo Man / Woman / Lady / Doctor: A person who practices hoodoo professionally, for pay, donations, or gratis, on behalf of others.

Jinx: A spell that leads to a loss of luck; it is less severe than crossing.

Job or Job of Work: A spell in the hoodoo tradition. It can also refer to a professional worker taking on spell-work for a client, for a specific condition, the extent and cost of which is agreed upon ahead of time.

Laying Tricks: Creating spell-work to be deployed in such a way that it will be contacted, touched, or walked over.

Lights: Oil lamps or candles are called lights; "setting lights" refers to working stationary candle or oil lamp spells over a series of days; "burning candles" is sometimes a euphemism for practicing hoodoo.

Messing Someone Up: Similar to crossing, messing someone up is commonly done by using physical powders that create a spiritual "mess."

Mojo: A small charm-bag, also called a toby, jomo, or gri-gri.

Nation Sack: A mojo made for a woman's power over her mate.

Nature: Can refer to sexuality generally, but is often meant to designate libido specifically; both men and women have nature.

Personal Concerns: A magical link to a person, such as hair, nails, foot-track dirt, sweat, sexual fluids, saliva, handwriting, or photos. If the target is a place, its "concerns" include dirt, mortar, splinters, maps, or photos.

Practitioner: A person who practices hoodoo; the term encompasses both home practitioners and professional root doctors.

Root Doctor: See Hoodoo Man / Woman / Lady / Doctor.

Roots, Rootwork: See Hoodoo.

Satisfaction: Obtaining the results desired.

Situation: See Condition.

Smoking: Suffumigating a person or place with incense.

Spiritual Supplies, Condition Products: Herbs, roots, minerals, oils, powders, incenses, candles, amulets, and curios, either home-made by a practitioner or purchased from a spiritual supply hous e.

Spiritual Supply House, Order House: Mail-order or online establishment through which spiritual supplies are purchased. In the past, many such companies also fielded door-to-door sales representatives.

Sprinkling and Blowing: Methods used to lay down sachet powders, mineral dusts, or herbs to be walked on or to be swept or vacuumed up.

Throwing Roots: See Working Roots.

Two-headed Doctor: See Hoodoo Man / Woman / Lady / Doctor.

Tying a Person's Nature: Making a person unable to perform sexually outside a given relationship; usually achieved through taking the person's (genital) measure, or by means of a nation sack.

Uncrossing: The act of taking off crossed conditions.

Working Roots: Casting a spell with roots or herbs. Like the term "burning candles," it is now also a euphemism for practicing hoodoo.

TRADITIONAL TOOLS AND METHODS

These are the basic supplies and techniques of African-American conjure. This list tells you why and when to use them and directs you to published books and free online resources that cover each subject in detail:

- **Baths and Floor Washes:** Bathing and washing are effective methods for uncrossing, cleansing, and drawing luck. Herb and mineral baths soothe excesses of emotion and are useful preludes to other spell-work.
  "Hoodoo Spiritual Baths" by Aura Laforest
  LuckyMojo.com/baths.html by Catherine Yronwode

- **Bible:** A source of inspiration and prayer, the Bible's textual passages, as well as the book itself, are widely employed by hoodoo practitioners.
  "Hoodoo Bible Magic" by Miss Michæle and Prof. C. D. Porterfield
  "Secrets of the Psalms" by Godfrey A. Selig
  ReadersAndRootWorkers.org/wiki/Category:The Book of Psalms

- **Bottle Spells:** A jar or bottle confines the work to a specific space. The bottle may be kept on an altar, shaken, buried, or otherwise deployed.
  LuckyMojo.com/bottlespells.html by Catherine Yronwode

- **Candle Work:** Candles heat things up, kindle passion, attract love or money, bring healing, enflame anger, or cause pain, as the worker chooses.
  "The Art of Hoodoo Candle Magic" by C. Yronwode and M. Strabo
  "The Master Book of Candle Burning" by Henri Gamache
  "The Guiding Light to Power and Success" by Mikhail Strabo
  "The Magic Candle" by Charmaine Dey
  "Candle Burning Magic: Rituals for Good and Evil" by Anna Riva
  LuckyMojo.com/candlemagic.html by Catherine Yronwode

- **Doll-Babies:** A doll or poppet is a magical effigy of someone made from wax, corn husks, clay, fabric, bread, leather, ceramics, or even plastic. It is spoken to and treated as the person would be. Dolls may be used for love, healing, binding, reversing, cursing, or other conditions.
  "The Black Folder" edited by Catherine Yronwode

• **Foot-Track Spells:** These spells include the deployment of herbs, roots, markings, or spiritual supplies so that they will come in contact with a person's footprints or be walked over. The dust from a person's foot-track may also be physically lifted and used as a personal concern in a spell.
LuckyMojo.com/foottrack.html by Catherine Yronwode

• **Freezer Spells:** These works bring matters to a halt, leave someone out in the cold, or stop them in their tracks by literally and figuratively putting things on ice. Often used when words need to be silenced, they can be worked with any fluid that will freeze, such as water or Lemon juice, and may also include selected fruits, vegetables, and animal parts.
LuckyMojo.com/freezer.html by Catherine Yronwode

• **Herbs, Roots, and Curios:** These are the building blocks of most spells and spiritual supplies. Each one's magical attributes and spirit work together for the purpose of effecting change and acting on a condition.
"Hoodoo Herb and Root Magic" by Catherine Yronwode
HerbMagic.com by Catherine Yronwode

• **Honey and Sugar Spells:** Sweet spells are employed when more sweetness, favours, or good intentions are required between two or more people. If worked in a container, they may continue for months or years.
"Hoodoo Honey and Sugar Spells" by Deacon Millett
LuckyMojo.com/honeyjar.html by Catherine Yronwode

• **Incense:** Condition-related and commercial incense blends are used in magical, religious, and altar work in thanks or as a blessing. In spell-casting, incense affects the mind. enhances work pertaining to speech, and is used to smoke objects and fix them prior to giving them to someone.
"Magic With Incense and Powders" by Anna Riva
LuckyMojo.com/incense.html by Catherine Yronwode

• **Jack Balls:** A jack is a specific type of toby made of thread or string wrapped around a core of personal concerns and magical items, usually worked for luck and personal power. It has a "tail" from which it is suspended, making it also suitable to use as a pendulum for divination.
Southern-Spirits.com/owen-hoodoo-luck-balls.html

- **Mirror Spells:** Mirrors reverse actions, spells, or thoughts back to the sender. These spells can be worked between two flat mirrors or in a mirror-lined box into which personal concerns, a packet, or a doll-baby is placed.
  LuckyMojo.com/reversing.html by Catherine Yronwode
  "The Black Folder" edited by Catherine Yronwode

- **Mojo Bags, Hands, Tobies, Jomos, Nation Sacks, Packets:** Herbs, roots, minerals, curios, and personal concerns tied or sewn into cloth or leather, or folded into a paper, these are spiritual spells worn on the person or fixed in a place and kept alive by feeding them oil, whiskey, or cologne.
  LuckyMojo.com/mojo.html
  LuckyMojo.com/jomo.html
  LuckyMojo.com/nationsack.html
  "Paper in My Shoe" by Catherine Yronwode
  "The Black Folder" edited by Catherine Yronwode

- **Condition Oils:** Essential or fragrance oils, plus herbs, roots, and minerals, prayerfully blended in an appropriate carrier oil, they are used to anoint the body, feed mojos, and dress candles or other objects.
  "Golden Secrets of Mystic Oils" by Anna Riva
  LuckyMojo.com/oils.html
  LuckyMojo.com/essentialoils.html
  LuckyMojo.com/oilblends.html

- **Personal Concerns:** Items taken from a person's body or touched during the course of daily life are used as links to them during spell-work.
  "Hoodoo Herb and Root Magic" by Catherine Yronwode

- **Petition, Prayer, and Name Papers:** Written papers are used to create a magical link to a person, or to express an intention, desire, or prayer.
  "Paper in My Shoe" by Catherine Yronwode

- **Sachet Powders:** Herbs, roots, minerals, and essential or fragrance oils, prayerfully blended in a powder base; they are sprinkled or blown in rooms or outdoors, used to draw altar designs, and to dust the body.
  "Magic with Incense and Powders" by Anna Riva
  LuckyMojo.com/powders.html by Catherine Yronwode

BEFORE YOU START

The best magical ingredients, tools, and techniques to use are those that are best suited to your specific situation — there is no "strongest spell." Start by honestly evaluating what needs to be done and work accordingly. To do that, ask yourself the following questions:

- **What kind of work am I doing?**
- **What personal concerns have axquired?**
- **Do I have access to the person(s) or their property?**
- **Do I want to affect the person's body, mind, nature, or situation?**
- **How complex is the situation?**
- **How long has the situation been going on?**
- **Is it a recurrent situation?**

Your answers to those questions will help you select the tools and techniques most likely to bring you satisfaction. They will help you assess which mundane actions will support your spiritual work. Finally, they will help establish how much work is needed and for how long.

A JOB OF WORK, INDEED

Casting a spell is a bit like an earth-moving operation. If all there is to move is a pebble, then a tiny push is all you need, perhaps a candle and a prayer. If there are many stones to move, things get more demanding. You may set a run of lights, plus a honey jar, worked over several weeks. What if there's a boulder in the way? If it's too big, it might need to be broken into pieces, each of which is taken care of separately. The job might require the help of a root doctor and spells including baths, candles, and a mojo hand. Then there's the sheer face of rock, a mountain, between you and your goal. There are a couple of alternatives in that of case: build a winding road around the mountain to where you want to go, or blast your way through it. Both choices will take time, work, and dedication — you're in for the long haul with no guarantees of success and lots of surprises on the road through to the unknown. You might even be best advised to backtrack and move in a different direction altogether.

WORKING FOR YOURSELF OR HIRING IT DONE

You have the choice of practicing hoodoo yourself, hiring it done, or a combination of the two. These factors may influence your decision:

- **Are your goals clear?** Rootworkers are exterior observers who can see what's going on, and because of their experience, they may assess the spell-work to be performed with more accuracy than you can.
- **Are you gifted for the type of work you're doing?** Most women do their own best love work, especially when sexual fluids are employed, but many hire a root doctor to assist in a child custody case.
- **Do you trust your spell-working knowledge?** If you fret about how to dress and pray over candles, or how to choose the right time to light them, a worker can explain traditional conjure with step-by-step detail.
- **Are you an "over-thinker"?** Obsessing over love and reconciliation jobs can be a problem. If you anxiously contact the person again and again, or if you contradict your love spell by picking fights or acting cold, your work will probably fail. Hire a worker to do the job while you take time to nurture yourself and address the roots of the problem.
- **Do you have the time and space to cast spells?** Women with a heavy workload or who lack privacy at home may not find it feasible to set lights over many days or use obvious spiritual supplies. Hire a helper, and follow through on any baths, teas, or contact work prescribed.
- **Do you have the money to hire a worker?** A reading is money well spent. Hiring a worker as a magical coach costs little more, except that it may take a few sessions. Buying or crafting your own rootwork supplies is economical. If you want a complete spell-casting service, be prepared to spend at least a week's wages.

Do some research before deciding who to work with and to what extent. Magical practitioners run the gamut from gifted professionals to shady scam artists. Check your worker's credentials; get a reading to see if the two of you connect. Ask for a written contract with prices, duration of the work, and number of contacts to be scheduled during the set time. Anyone new to hiring a spiritual worker should read these web pages:
LuckyMojo.com/blackgypsies.html
ReadersAndRootworkers.org/wiki/Suggestions_For_Clients

UPHOLDING THE MAGICAL WITH THE MUNDANE

Throughout this book, I urge you to back up magic spells with worldly work, and vice versa. A couple of examples will clarify what this means:

EXAMPLE 1: A BANK LOAN TO CONSOLIDATE DEBT

Let's say you need a bank loan to consolidate your debt, which consists of utility bills, unplanned home repairs, and credit card bills. This debt has been building for the past five years, since moving into a home in a fancier part of town. You could work for the loan using a sweet jar or coercive candle on the financial institution or bank manager. This is a valid way of getting a loan, but the results may be short-lived because the root of the problem has not been addressed. New unplanned repairs will crop up, the utility bills will be back next month, and the desire to keep up with the neighbours will lead to upward-creeping credit card balances. So, yes, work the sweet jar on the bank, but combine it with the following steps:

MAGICAL LOAN-GETTING WORK

• **Spiritual House-Cleaning:** Use Chinese Wash and Van Van Incense to turn bad luck to good and clear out the "stink of debt" in the home.

• **Candle Magic:** Set Money House Blessing and Money Stay With Me Vigil Lights in the kitchen or living room the first Sunday of every month.

• **Herbal Allies:** Grow and maintain both Basil and Thyme plants in the kitchen window, or in a window near the front door.

• **A Mojo Hand:** Keep a small, sewn, flat packet of Alfalfa, Five-Finger Grass and Fenugreek with a petition paper in your wallet.

MUNDANE DEBT-REDUCING WORK

• **Make a Budget:** Consult a financial advisor or community finance organization to plan a budget that includes savings for future expenses.

• **Re-Think Credit Card Use:** This can be done with the help of a credit counselling agency. Perhaps a debit card would be more suitable.

• **Assess Your Lifestyle:** If you are living above the current financial means available, be ready to make changes such as moving or downsizing vehicles, wardrobe, and appliances if necessary.

• **Increase Your Income:** Bring in more income through job promotion or transfer, by taking a part-time job, or by starting a cottage industry.

EXAMPLE 2: KEEPING AN ABSENT LOVER FAITHFUL

Your lover will be working overseas for the next six months. You've lived together for two years, but your lover has a wandering eye and you are worried about fidelity. Prior to the person's departure, spell-work was not done, nor were personal concerns secured, but you found some residual hair. You want your lover to come home without having had an outside affair. Ideally, to secure sexual fidelity, a nation sack or some other method of tying your lover's nature would have been undertaken before the journey was announced. Given the impossibility of working in the past, however, there are a number of approaches that can be taken in the present to aid in obtaining the desired outcome:

MAGICAL LONG-DISTANCE FIDELITY WORK

• **Vigil Lights:** Set Safe Travel and Return To Me Vigil Candles over your partner's name at least once a month, and once a week if possible.

• **Skull Candles and Incense:** Convey messages of love and fidelity with a red skull loaded with your lover's hair and love herbs. Burn it in sections, with a mix of Tobacco and Return To Me incense on the side.

• **Sneaky Food Tricks:** Look for snacks with sulphur, sulphate, or sulphite in the preservatives. Pray over the food for faithfulness and send them in a "care package." The sulphur will help tie your lover's nature.

• **Dress All Gifts:** Regularly send interesting, unusual, and thoughtful items. These can be secretly dressed with your sweat or juices.

• **Fix Gifts of Clothing:** Send a cap in one of your care packages. Sew your pubic hairs into the head-band to stay on your lover's mind.

• **Ask the Ants to Bring Your Loved One Back:** Go to a Red Ants' nest at sunrise, call his name three times, ask the Ants to tell him to come home.

MUNDANE WORK FOR LONG-DISTANCE CONNECTIONS

• **Maintain Regular Contact:** Use the phone, email, texts, and letters to stay in touch. Send photos frequently. If responses dwindle or response-times increase, keep your temper and maintain your regular pace.

• **Engage in Sexual Intimacy:** Regular Skype calls that include net-sex will keep your absent lover's libido well cared for. This reduces straying or resorting to the use of impersonal pornography.

• **Plan Together:** Plan activities to be shared upon your lover's return. Begin to make them a reality and keep your lover aware of developments.

OBSTACLES TO SUCCESSFUL SPELL-WORK

Without a reading, we cannot diagnose "what went wrong" on any given spell, but here are some common obstacles and problems.

WAITING TOO LONG ... OR NOT LONG ENOUGH

"How long should I work?" and "When should I give up?" are questions whose answers vary. Consider \the legnth of your life-span, how long the negative condition existed, and how late you started to fix it — and always set a time limit on work intended to change a person's mind.

LACKING CLARITY AND PRECISION IN YOUR PETITION

When you're unclear or unspecific about what the desired outcome to be obtained actually is, the results can be unpredictable. For example, a candle spell requesting "more customers" or "more sales" may bring one extra person a day to your store ... buying a one dollar item. Technically the spell is a success, but the end result is probably not what you were looking for. Specifying a weekly dollar amount or an amount by which the weekly sales figures increase could have yielded more satisfying results.

BEING OF TWO MINDS OR CONTRADICTING THE WORK

Being of two minds is typical in many love reconciliation situations. On the one hand, a woman wants to get her ex-lover back, but on the other hand, she's still angry and wants the ex to suffer. In a situation like this, she might do impeccable magical work to return the ex, while her mundane behaviour oscillates between sweetness and nit-picking fights. Even worse is the woman who magically works against her own magic, feeding the ex menses-laced sugar cookies, while at the same time torturing him with a run of Intranquil Spirit Candles. Your work and your life are extensions of your mind, and if your mind is divided, your work will not stand.

INCONSISTENT APPLICATION OF EFFORT

When tasks like setting lights on honey jars, feeding a mojo hand, or taking a run of spiritual baths fall by the wayside, results may dwindle away, because the message being sent to the universe is that your spells (and the results they are meant to manifest) are unimportant. If you skip a day of work, just pick up where you left off, but do try harder next time.

NOT THINKING THE MUNDANE OUTCOME THROUGH

"Be careful what you wish for because you just might get it" is an old cliché, but also wise advice. Imagine using a Steady Work Spell Kit to get a higher-paying job, but not accounting for a longer commute, higher taxes, and mean new co-workers. The new job amounts to pretty much the same as the last one, except that now you no longer have seniority, you have no friends at work, and it's a year until your next vacation. Too bad!

BATTLING AN OPPONENT OR ENEMY TO YOUR WORK

As Miss cat says, "There are two kinds of spells or prayers. The first is the farmer's prayer: *'Lord, I have plowed and planted good seed, now I pray that you send regular rain to make the crop grow, and stop the rain when it is time for me to harvest. Amen.'* There is no enemy and no opposition, just you and God. The second is the boxer's prayer: *'O Lord, let me get up there tonight and beat the crap out of the other guy.'* The problem is, the other guy may have been praying hard too. Your chance of winning is helped if he didn't do any spiritual work, but if he comes at you righteous and carrying roots, you will have a tougher fight on your hands. And always remember, in break-up situations, it's not just you versus the other woman. If children are involved, they are praying, *'God, don't make Mommy and Daddy get a divorce.'* And God listens to their prayers too."

"BREAKING" A GOOD OLD TRADITIONAL SPELL

Hoodoo spells are time-tested recipes from a long, living tradition in the African-American community. Rewriting the way in which the work is done because bathing at dawn is inconvenient, or substituting a different herb to save a dollar is just giving yourself trouble and failure for nothing. There are hundreds of excellent conjure spells that will not require radical alteration to suit your situation or your lifestyle. Choose another one.

FAILURE TO TRUST IN SPIRIT

When sincere and justified spells fail, the seeming failure may be a lesson we are meant to learn or may open a new path for us to step out on. The man we tried to marry may be a child abuser; the person we cursed to death may have a role to play as a hero later on. Trusting Spirit, God, Divinity, or the Universe when our desires are not granted can be difficult, but ultimately life leads us where we're meant to go.

THE STAGES OF OUR LIVES

A WOMAN'S JOURNEY

Let's look at the issues which affect our lives as women and develop integrated magical and mundane strategies for success. Not every woman will experience all of these situations — but for every stage of life, there are traditional hoodoo spells, and we can use them for our benefit.

- **The Young Woman:** We overcome the disadvantages of poor parenting, school bullying, negative conditioning about our bodies, and the bad effects of succumbing to peer pressure.
- **The Independent Woman:** We build self-confidence and self-esteem, acquire charisma, embark upon a career, and win respect in society, which leads to a lifetime of financial stability.
- **The Lover:** We seek romance, love and sex. Using all the secrets of female conjure, we attract and charm a mate, and we learn to return love and hold it dear. And some of us seek marriage.
- **The Wife:** We set up a household with our lover, and we assume the duties, joys, and responsibilities of maintaining a spiritually clean, tranquil, and peaceful home that helps us hold on to what we've got.
- **The Mother:** We become pregnant, give birth, and nurture our little ones, making use of age-old magical methods to keep the children safe, secure, and thriving in a supportive family environment.
- **The Grandmother:** We foster the perpetuation of our historical lineage through the generations, spreading love to our grandchildren and offering wise counsel to our family and our culture.
- **The Widow:** We may suffer the loss of a spouse, and although there is no "best" way to deal with grief or loneliness, a few techniques have been known to help and are offered with love.
- **Starting Over:** At any stage in life we may have to begin some situations over. We may wish to reunite after a break up or negotiate the path of divorce and remarriage. Let us do so gracefully.
- **The Hoodoo Lady:** We have a few tricks up our sleeves as we undertake magic on behalf of others, freeing the innocent from evil work or, if necessary, bringing justice to those who have done wrong.

Spiritual products for love, marriage, and peace in the home, 1929 - 2017. Art by Charles C. Dawson, R. C. Adams, K. Rudin, and three Unknown Artists for Famous Products, Oracle Products, R. C. Adams, and Lucky Mojo Curio Co.

ᴛʜᴇ Yᴏᴜɴɢ Wᴏᴍᴀɴ

RESOLVING FEMALE GUILT AND SHAME

Guilt isn't necessarily a problem, but if it turns into shame it usually will become one. Guilt and shame are constructs which, historically, have served to maintain cultural norms and promote cohesive behaviour within a social group or community. Shaming was one of the first forms of non-violent group discipline and its power still echoes deep within our psyche.

We women often feel shame and guilt over things that are not our fault to begin with and also over things that different societies may not find shameful. What we have done in the past, how we have reacted to certain situations, how we felt about specific experiences, and even how we look can all be sources of self-discomfort, anxiety, or depression. If shame becomes internalized and we think *"I am bad"* rather than *"I did something bad,"* our ability to function can be severely compromised.

Common origins of female shame include gender identification; sexual preference; accepting the false belief that we "permitted" or "allowed" ourselves to become victims of a sex crime, incest, rape, or domestic abuse; having been bullied; weight gain; the inability to attain an idealized body shape; having an eating disorder; failure to keep an even temper; failure to overcome addictions; having a mental illness; having a criminal record; having had an abortion; the belief that by not paying attention to warning signs we were "at fault" for a miscarriage; giving a child up for adoption; being an unwed mother; not being able to keep a father in our children's lives; having a child taken away by protective services; being a single mom who doesn't earn enough money to keep the children well clothed; being homeless; inability to care for our elderly parents; and failure to warn or save a friend or relative who died young. That's quite a list, and most women reading this can probably think of many more!

Ending the vicious circle of self-shame requires walking away from it. Be it easy or difficult to identify the causes of our shame, as long as we walk down the same mental path we have always taken, the end result is that we will invariably return to our self-shame. However, if we start to take baby steps in a different direction toward self-forgiveness and self-compassion, eventually we find that we're on a new path altogether.

SELF-FORGIVENESS AND SELF-COMPASSION

Self-forgiveness and self-compassion are critical components of moving out of the jail cell that guilt and shame can build around us. Only through forgiveness of the past and willingness to walk open-heartedly into the future do we create a moment of change in the present. Help may be necessary as we learn to practice self-forgiveness and self-compassion. Support groups, social workers, therapists, ministers, and community organizations are good mundane places to look when undertaking healing. A close friend, a trusted mentor, or a family member can be another alternative. If you wish to undertake the process independently or anonymously, there are excellent self-help books and online forums addressing a variety of shame-causing situations.

Shame transformed is not cynical hardness; it is self-respect and justifiable pride. We don't need to be happy with all we are, or proud of all we have done to accept who we are. Self-acceptance allows us to renew ourselves and spark movement and change in both thought and action.

HERBS THAT RESOLVE GUILT AND SHAME
- **Althæa leaf:** Eases painful memories by soothing and healing.
- **Fennel:** Gives courage to women and keeps bad influences away.
- **Hops:** Brings restful sleep, free from traumatic dreams of the past.
- **Hyssop:** Removes real or perceived sins and transgressions. Helps assuage guilt over past actions and thoughts.
- **Mint:** Provides cooling, protective mental strength and clarity.
- **Yarrow:** For courage to face hard situations, memories, and people.

SPIRITUAL SUPPLIES THAT RESOLVE GUILT AND SHAME
- **Cast Off Evil:** Does away with unwanted habits, thoughts, or actions and keeps away bad influences.
- **Clarity:** Opens the eyes to the truth and enables insight; were you to blame, or was it society or an evil person?
- **Crucible of Courage:** Fosters the necessary strength to face sensitive or hurtful situations and embark on changes.
- **Cut and Clear:** Breaks links to past people and social groups.
- **Healing:** Helps heal pains of all kinds.
- **John the Conqueror:** Overcomes weakness with strength.

PRAYERS TO RESOLVE GUILT OR SHAME

Prayer is a powerful aid to change. These scriptures deal with overcoming shame and guilt, and finding forgiveness for past misdeeds. If you prefer to pray from your own heart in your own words, that is perfectly fine as well, as are other methods of self-transformation, such as visualization, affirmations, and meditation.

- **Psalms 51:1-2:** *"Have mercy upon me, O God, according to thy lovingkindness: according unto the multitude of thy tender mercies blot out my transgressions. Wash me thoroughly from mine iniquity, and cleanse me from my sin."* (The entire Psalm is generally recited when bathing with Hyssop and drinking Hyssop tea.)
- **Psalms 103:11-12:** *"For as the heaven is high above the Earth, so great is his mercy toward them that fear him. As far as the East is from the West, so far hath he removed our transgressions from us."*
- **Proverbs 28:13:** *"He that covereth his sins shall not prosper: but whoso confesseth and forsaketh them shall have mercy."*
- **Isaiah 43:25:** *"I, even I, am he that blotteth out thy transgressions for mine own sake, and will not remember thy sins."*
- **Romans 3:23:** *"For all have sinned, and come short of the glory of God."*
- **Philippians 4:13:** *"I can do all things through Christ which strengtheneth me."*
- **1 John 1:9:** *"If we confess our sins, he is faithful and just to forgive us our sins, and to cleanse us from all unrighteousness."*
- **Revelations 21:4:** *"And God shall wipe away all tears from their eyes; and there shall be no more death, neither sorrow, nor crying, neither shall there be any more pain: for the former things are passed away."*

A TOBY FOR SELF-HEALING AND SELF-COMPASSION

In a red flannel bag on which is sewn a small cross, place a whole Angelica Root, oiled with Blessing or Healing oils, a pinch of All-Heal herb, a pinch of Althæa herb. and a name paper into which is folded a lock of your hair. Smoke the bag in Healing Incense and pray your prayers into it before tying it shut. Feed it with Healing Oil once a week, on Mondays.

CLEANSING AWAY ANXIETY AND SHAME

Virtually every form of cleansing can be brought into play as you move beyond youthful shame or guilt. Hands-on cleansing is a potent way to start the process off, especially for those who have access to a local root doctor who can perform the work in person. Baths wash away the pain and the negative emotionsal residues from bad experiences.

Smoking or suffumigating a person in cleansing or healing incense and regularly burning or spraying uplifting scents in the home is another favourite technique to help resolve complex situations of guilt and shame. This should be done regularly, over time, to yield the best results.

FORGIVENESS FROM SIN BATH

If you feel shame for what you have done, bathe in a strong tea of Hyssop while praying Psalms 51. Reserve a cup of weak Hyssop tea to drink (unless you are pregnant, in which case forego the tea).

HERBAL BATH FOR PERSONAL FORGIVENESS

Combine two parts Hyssop, one part Yarrow, and one part of either Blessed Thistle or Yerba Santa. Brew this into a spiritual bath to be taken before sunrise. Pray Psalms 51 during the bath. Dispose of some of the used bath water toward the rising Sun.

BATH FOR CLARITY IN TIMES OF TURMOIL

Combine eight parts Mint, four part Pine needles, two parts Eucalyptus leaf, one part Sage, and four parts kosher salt. Brew the herbs into a strong tea and dissolve the salt in the hot tea. Wash the head with this mixture before sunrise daily for three days. Dispose of some of the used bath water toward the rising Sun.

BLUE BATH TO REMOVE NEGATIVE ENERGY

If a sense of guilt or shame has driven you into a deep feeling of sadness, dissolve a square of Reckitt's Crown Blue or a Blue Anil Ball in a pot of very hot water, add 1 teaspoon of Lemon juice and a few drops of Van Van Oil, and dilute this into a bathtub of warm water for bathing. If you wish, you may also use it for washing off any object that you feel has been touched by a negative person, including any amulets, crystals, or talismans of yours that have lost their energy.

DEALING WITH BAD HABITS AND ADDICTION

Addictions and bad habits have genetic and behavioural components, and they are also linked in some cases to mental illness. It is generally among young and newly independent women that temptations and dependencies first are seen for what they are. If not handled promptly, these youthful inclinations can lead to a lifetime of suffering, because addicts often fail to reach the enjoyable milestones of life achieved by those who through good luck, earnest prayer, fortunate family training, a genetic inclination to avoid risks, adherence to moral principles, or learning through observation of bad examples avoided the pitfalls of addiction.

Our addictions may be linked to guilt and shame. If addictive dependencies developed as coping methods during times of trauma, the guilt and shame is twofold: once for not being able to deal with the trauma and once for the trap we sprung on ourselves while trying to cope.

Completely cutting off life-threatening addictions such as drug and alcohol abuse is the surest form of sobriety and recovery. The anorexic or binge eater, however, cannot forego food completely and will need to find healthy ways to relate to it over the long term. What we seek in these instances is not a "cold turkey" cessation of the damaging behaviour, but harm reduction, learning to walk the tightrope between too much and not enough, and a way to travel on the middle path between extremes.

Although in all magical work it is important to address the mundane, this is particularly true when dealing with issues of addiction. Help can take many forms, including peer-led recovery groups, residential rehab centers, community health clinics, faith-based communities, or psychiatric medical therapists. Books and online discussion forums can be of some aid, but when an addiction is serious, local in-person help should be sought out.

If you are struggling with addiction or bad habits, both the mundane and magical work you will need is best undertaken by you, on your own behalf, rather than being hired out to a root doctor. Only you can take the first steps necessary to change yourself.

If addictions that plague the life of someone close to you affect your happiness or safety, often the best decision you can make is to save yourself. Get whatever help you need to move away and come to terms with the fact that the other person's addiction was not your fault.

HERBS FOR DEALING WITH ADDICTIONS

- **Angelica Root:** A strong guardian in times of crisis.
- **Bay Leaf:** Clears the mind and brings both insight and wisdom.
- **Black Walnut:** Kills off desire for no-good things or people.
- **Eucalyptus:** Gives strength to stay away from evil temptations, people, or places; helps one breathe easier when thoughts or sensations within the body are oppressive.
- **Goldenseal:** Improves health and nurtures beauty, strength and wisdom, making it easier to leave old hurtful habits behind; often used in conjunction with Holy Ghost Root (Angelica).
- **John the Conqueror Root:** Fosters the strength, personal mastery, and energy needed to overcome obstacles; it combines well with Master of the Woods for this purpose.
- **Knotweed (Ladies Thumb):** Ties down things to be cast away.
- **Lemon:** Clears away spiritual dross and refreshes the mind.
- **Master of the Woods:** Increases our energy to overcome obstacles; it combines well with John the Conqueror for this purpose.
- **Sage:** Purifies, gives strength to women, and imparts wisdom.
- **Salt:** Sends away evil and protects against its return.

SPIRITUAL SUPPLIES FOR ADDICTION ISSUES

- **Blessing:** Encourages divine intervention and offsets the inner critic, harshness, and blame which can come up during recovery.
- **Blueing:** For blue baths, which have a soothing and calming quality well-suited to the agitation that often accompanies addiction issues.
- **Cast Off Evil:** Helps remove bad habits, addictions, and troubling behaviour; also used to get rid of negative people and influences.
- **Cut and Clear:** To make a clean break with the past.
- **Healing:** Aids in physical, mental and spiritual recovery.
- **Holy Water:** Invites divine intervention and angelic assistance.
- **Rose of Crucifixion:** Excellent when mental turmoil or anguish is problematic; to soothe and quiet the mind in conjunction with faith.
- **Run Devil Run:** To send away bad habits. This formula seems to work quite well on hard alcohol ("spirits") as well as drug issues, or when a particularly "devilish" person is acting as an evil influence.
- **Tranquility:** For serenity and calm while dealing with inner mental issues and with negative people who encourage addictive behaviours.

CANDLE SPELL TO FIND THE MIDDLE PATH

Prepare a small table or bureau top as a work or altar space. On one side, lay a small Bible to Matthew 7:13-14 *("Enter through the narrow gate; for the gate is wide and the way is broad that leads to destruction, and there are many who enter through it. For the gate is small and the way is narrow that leads to life, and there are few who find it.")*

Print out two images of the tarot card of The Devil and glue one onto each of two unlabelled black glass-encased candles. Print out one image of the tarot card of The Sun and glue it onto an unlabelled orange vigil light.

On a petition paper, write your name nine times, then rotate the paper 90 degrees clockwise and cover and cross your name with *"I walk the middle road"* nine times. Five-spot the paper with Road Opener and Crucible of Courage oils and fold it in half, toward you, adding a couple of hairs from your head as you do so. Place it beneath the orange candle.

Make the Clarity Incense into cones and set them on a small fire-proof surface or in a shallow bowl filled with salt at the center of the work space. Light the incense. Read Matthew 7:13-14 aloud and set it down, still open on the work space, just in front of the incense.

Dress the black candles with finely-cut Eucalyptus leaves and Banishing Oil. As you fix each candle say, *"Remove the shackles that bind me, the evil influences that restrain me, and help me find the small gate and narrow way that lead to the middle path."*

Place the black candles at the bottom right and bottom left of an imaginary triangle whose apex points upwards and encloses the Bible and incense within its limits. The Bible and incense should be in the center. Light the candles and read again Matthew 7:13-14.

Dress the orange candle with a mixture of finely-cut Lemongrass, Althæa, and Yarrow herbs, plus Road Opener and Crucible of Courage Oils. As you fix the candle say, *"I have found and walk the middle road. When I fall off the path, I return again to the middle road. The right path is open in front of me."*

Place the candle at the apex of the imaginary triangle. Light the candle and read again Matthew 7:13-14.

If desired, light incense and read the verse from Matthew daily during the duration of the candle burn. When the candles have gone out, recycle the glass and bury the incense ashes and petition paper at the base of a large, old tree — an Oak or Willow if possible.

HEALING BLUE BATH FOR ADDICTION ISSUES

Mix a crushed square of Reckitt's Crown Blue; a cup of Salt, and a splash of Holy Water in a full tub of hot water. Pray 1 Corinthians 6:12 (*"All things are lawful unto me, but all things are not expedient: all things are lawful for me, but I will not be brought under the power of any."*) during the bath. Soak for 20 minutes, washing downward from head to toe. Air-dry and dress in clean clothes. Dispose of some of the used bath water in a crossroads toward the setting Sun and return home without looking back.

A HAND FOR OVERCOMING BAD HABITS

Combine a small John the Conqueror Root, a pinch of Yarrow, a pinch of White Oak bark chips, and a pinch of Blessed Thistle in a red flannel bag. Add your name paper with your hairs in it, folded towards you. Feed it weekly with a blend of John the Conqueror and Rose of Crucifixion oils.

BATH CRYSTAL BLEND FOR FIGHTING TEMPTATION

Combine equal parts Cast Off Evil Bath Crystals, Eucalyptus Bath Crystals, and Run Devil Run Bath Crystals in a tub of water. Soak for 20 minutes, washing downward from head to toe. During the bath, pray 1 Corinthians 10:13 (*"God is faithful, who will not suffer you to be tempted above that ye are able; but will with the temptation also make a way to escape, that ye may be able to bear it."*) Dispose of some of the used bath water in a crossroads toward the setting Sun and walk away.

WALNUT, EUCALYPTUS, AND LEMON TO BREAK A HABIT

Boil up a bath-tea with one Black or English Walnut, still in its shell, plus a handful of Eucalyptus leaves. Strain the liquid and add the juice of one Lemon. Freeze the liquid in cubes, then dissolve and dilute as needed. Adding a cube to a hot bath once a week helps to drive off wicked companions and put a stop to tobacco, drug, or alcohol dependency.

KNOTWEED TO TIE DOWN TOBACCO OR MARIJUANA

Mix Knot Weed with soft wax and roll it around a pinch of Marijuana or Tobacco, forming a ball. On a piece of paper, write your desire for Tobacco or Marijuana to die out of your life, wrap the paper around the ball, and tie it with a mop string. Bury the ball in a graveyard, asking the dead to tie down your problem until you return; then walk away.

MENTAL DISTRESS AND MENTAL ILLNESS

Mental distress and emotional difficulties can can make even the simplest of activities challenging, agonizing, or outright impossible. If you struggle with a mental conditon such as obsessive compulsive disorder, anxiety, panic attacks, depression, bipolar disorder, self-harming, or suicidal ideation, getting proper medical and social care is critical. Magic won't replace that, nor should it.

MUNDANE STRATEGIES TO EASE MENTAL DISTRESS

Chances are you know what to do already; most of these suggestions are common sense advice we simply need to put into practice:

- **Exercise:** Body movement, calisthenics, martial arts, weight training, dance, yoga, walking, and anything that either gets you sweating or controls your breathing will help change your brain balance.
- **Diet:** Malnourishment, nutrient deficiencies, obesity, and anorexia harm health and well-being. Better food will improve the mood.
- **Contact with Nature:** The texture, sounds, and sensations of nature relax body and mind, reminding us that we're part of a greater whole, a wondrous and tiny functioning piece of a larger ecosystem.
- **Prayer:** Spiritual faith in a higher power, angels, guardian spirits, or ancestors, no matter what one's religious tradition, has an uplifting effect on the mind and soothes the weary heart.
- **Meditation:** These age-old practices have survived the centuries because they work; in our fast-paced never-stop world they can be an island of calm which helps anchor the mind through its many storms.
- **Family and Social Activities:** It is a basic human need to be with other people and no amount of phoning, texting, or Skyping will ever replace warm-blooded human contact.
- **Community Involvement:** Working for something or someone outside ourselves while connecting with our sense of altruism and compassion helps put our own pain in perspective.
- **Professional Help:** Seeking the help of a trained therapist, family doctor, herbalist, naturopath, psychologist, or psychiatrist can help anyone who is dealing with and healing an unbalanced state of mind. Don't be shy or ashamed to consult a mental health professional.

SPIRITUAL BATHS FOR MENTAL DISTRESS

In times of trial, baths are particularly suitable since the water element speaks directly to the emotional state and also provides a soothing contact with the entire body. However, we usually have enough on our minds, so this is when quality pre-blended spiritual baths are a good idea. The time, energy and focus that we would spend determining which herbs to use can be bypassed and devoted instead to our healing. Meanwhile, the prayers of those making the supplies back up and support our recovery efforts.

- **Blessing:** Encourages divine intervention in efforts of healing. A really comforting formula, it wraps you up like a warm blanket and makes you feel like it will all be okay.
- **Clarity:** When upset clouds the mind and it becomes difficult to think clearly, this is the formula to turn to.
- **Crucible of Courage:** Brings the courage necessary to recognize difficult situations and the bravery to try to deal with them.
- **Healing:** Aids in physical, mental and spiritual recovery of all kinds.
- **Rose of Crucifixion:** Excellent when mental turmoil or anguish is particularly problematic; it works to soothe and quiet the mind.
- **Saint Dymphna:** For those who work with saints, she is of aid when mental illness or sexual abuse issues are present.
- **Tranquility:** Good for anxious states of mind or when there's difficulty relaxing or getting proper sleep.
- **Thirteen Herb Bath:** Removes accumulated negativity or anything magical that may have been thrown. Useful to break cycles of painful thought or fixed ideas which maintain distress.
- **Uncrossing:** Frees you from any curses or ill-wishes that may have added to your anguish.

COLTSFOOT INCENSE FOR MENTAL TROUBLES

Burning powdered Coltsfoot herb with Blessing Incense or Frankincense is an old prescription to remove both physical sickness and mental troubles.

NETTLE TO OVERCOME IRRATIONAL FEARS

On a small piece of paper write your present most urgent fears and cross them with your name nine times. Carry the paper in a small packet with a pinch each of Yarrow and Nettle, and you will gradually overcome these fears.

¶HE INDEPENDENT WOMAN

COMING INTO YOUR PERSONAL POWER

From puberty onward, we have one important spiritual task: to become self-empowered. Young womanhood can be a difficult time. The fragility of childhood has not yet been overcome but already we receive offers from peers to engage in risk-taking ventures. In the mundane world, we seek to gain physical dexterity, train our mental skills, overcome disadvantages, and develop strength of will, but spiritually, throughout this portion of our life journey, as we grow from childhood to womanhood, we meet with many tests and trials. It is good to remember that our trials are what make us grow, give us our depth, and allow us to know transfiguration and metamorphosis intimately, personally, directly.

Self-knowledge is the foundation for self-empowerment. It includes a sense of personal history, awareness of our strengths and shortcomings, likes and dislikes, abilities and limitations. The "self" is neither a static construct nor a planned facade. It isn't the skin of a chameleon which changes colour to suit its environment — it is instead more like a tree, growing but stable in its roots and comfortable in its space.

Self-work is the root of personal power and that power bears beautiful fruits: confidence, charisma, understanding, compassion, respect, and sincerity. It profoundly affects our world and our perceptions. Improving and nurturing personal power reverberates into all aspects of our lives.

Personal power is also the foundation of our magical work. Our belief in ourselves and what we deserve helps us manifest it in our lives. We need to know and believe we deserve the best and that we are able to make that happen for ourselves. From that belief, intent, focus, and clarity are possible as we move toward our chosen magical outcome.

For women, personal power work is particularly necessary, because taking our place in the sun can be difficult. The feminine voice, expression, and traditional range of activity have been de-valued. Only today are we women beginning to obtain a proper place in society. Like plants that creep their way back into cleared land, the Female Spirit is re-establishing Herself as opportunity and equality grow. However one chooses to be as a woman, this deserves to be celebrated.

BUILDING-BLOCKS OF SELF-EMPOWERMENT

Depending on the situations that have shaped us and the twists and turns that have characterized the walk of our lives, each of us has different areas that need more or less self-work on the path to our own personal power. Self-empowerment is crafted from the building blocks of self-confidence, self-esteem, and self-respect. These are related yet distinct states of mind. Each one affects the other and they can be worked on simultaneously or individually depending on the need.

- **Self-Confidence:** Conviction in one's ability to perform a task or activity. Authority, knowledge, and competence in a given field, expressed without undue arrogance: A "we can do it" attitude.
- **Self-Esteem:** The value assigned to the self, usually in comparison with others around us. Self-esteem is critical to a sense of belonging within a group or structure and in being comfortable as one is.
- **Self-Respect:** Knowledge of one's internal values and beliefs and consistency between this internal paradigm and external words and actions. Usually establishes the "limits" of what we'll accept or not.

When we possess and exhibit the qualities of self-confidence, self-esteem, and self-respect, we attract blessings to ourselves. We are up-beat and positive, surrounded and cherished by friends. We are magnetic, and we exhibit forceful will-power.

Read more about development of these qualities in this book:
Personal Codes of the Crystal Silence League by C. Alexander

FOR SELF-CONFIDENCE, SELF-ESTEEM, SELF-RESPECT
- **Black Cohosh Root:** Strengthens weak or timid people.
- **Bo' Hog Root:** To attract affection; to make a woman strong.
- **Deer's Tongue:** To find the right words to express yourself.
- **John the Conqueror Root:** To conquer fears, weakness, and doubt.
- **Master Root:** To gain control through authority and leadership.
- **Master of the Woods:** For victory in contests or among groups.
- **Queen Elizabeth Root:** For the strength to be a powerful woman.
- **Sampson Snake Root:** For strength and protection from enemies.
- **Sang (Ginseng) Root:** To enhance personal success and energy.

SPIRITUAL SUPPLIES FOR SELF-EMPOWERMENT

To select spiritual supplies for empowering yourself, look at the goals you've set and pick the formulas aligned with those qualities.

- **Empowerment as a Woman:**
  Queen Elizabeth Root in Oil, Power, and Crucible of Courage, plus added Rosemary, Yarrow, Fennel, and Queen Elizabeth Roots.
- **Empowerment in Embracing Change:**
  Van Van, Road Opener, Magnet, and Attraction, plus Crucible of Courage if feeling weak or Block Buster if feeling "stuck."
- **Empowerment in Employment:**
  Steady Work, Master, and John the Conqueror; Boss Fix and Stop Gossip may be added to these, if necessary.
- **Empowerment in Management:**
  Jupiter, Master, John the Conqueror, Power, plus added Licorice, Calamus, and Deer's Tongue.
- **Empowerment in Negotiations:**
  Influence, King Solomon Wisdom, Mercury, and Crown of Success, plus added Deer's Tongue.
- **Empowerment in Financial Matters:**
  Money Drawing, Money Stay With Me, and Crown of Success, in conjunction with a Lodestone or a magnet.
- **Empowerment in Sports Contests:**
  Nature, John the Conqueror, Power, and Victory.

A THREE-ROOT HAND FOR FEMALE SELF-CONFIDENCE

Magical items carried on the person increase self-confidence and provide a constant reminder of the work you are doing and the goals you wish to achieve. A single High John the Conqueror Root, dressed with John the Conqueror Oil and kept as a pocket piece is traditional, as is a single Queen Elizabeth Root dressed with Queen Elizabeth Root in Oil.

Another old-time favourite is a mojo hand consisting of three or more roots tied, wrapped, or sewn into red flannel. A three-root bag for self-confidence can be made with the two roots named above, plus a small whole Sang (Ginseng) root dressed with Power Oil — or with a Sang Root, plus a few pieces of Black Snake (Black Cohosh) Root, and a few slices of Bo' Hog (Lovage) Root, all three dressed with Power Oil.

HAND FOR PERSONAL POWER AND SELF-KNOWLEDGE

Place a large piece of Master Root, a large pinch of Master of the Woods herb, a large pinch of Sage, a few small pieces of Frankincense resin, and a small bundle of Pine needles tied together with thread in a red mojo bag. Add a name paper with your hairs in it, folded towards you. Tie the bag shut and feed it weekly with King Solomon Wisdom Oil.

TURNSTEEL'S HAND FOR FEMALE STRENGTH

"Combine a small Angelica Root, a piece of Dragon's Blood resin, a piece of Frankincense resin, a piece of Myrrh resin, a piece of Master Root, a piece of Lightning Struck Wood, and an Oak Gall in a black mojo bag. Add your own name paper with your hairs and a bit of gold leaf in it, folded towards you. Feed it every Sunday with whiskey. This hand will give the woman who owns it strength of body and spirit."

A WOMAN'S HAND FOR WISDOM AND MASTERY

Into a red mojo bag place a slice of Ginger Root, a slice of Angelica Root, a slice of Licorice Root, a slice of Solomon's Seal Root, a slice of Peony root, a piece of Master Root, and a piece of Sarsaparilla root. Feed it weekly with an appropriate condition oil and your own menstrual blood.

MAGDALYNA'S MIRACULOUS MEDAL HAND OF POWER

"Into a red mojo bag with a Miraculous Medal sewn to it, add a slice of Queen Elizabeth Root, a large pinch of Master of the Woods, a Cowrie shell, a small sprig of dried Rosemary, a slice of Angelica Root, your own dried menstrual blood, and a petition paper with your hairs in it, folded towards you. Tie or sew the bag shut. Wear the hand in your bra and feed it with Queen Elizabeth Root in Oil."

WOMEN'S EMPOWERMENT INCENSE BLEND

Write a petition for personal power and burn it to ash. Mix the ash with one packet each of Power Incense Powders, Queen Elizabeth Root Incense Powders, 1/4 teaspoon powdered Rosemary, and a pinch of your own dried and powdered menstrual blood. Burn daily until the mixture is completely used up. Dispose of the ashes in your front yard. This mixture can also be burnt during spells done for personal strength, for empowerment and in endeavours of female domination.

WINNING THE RESPECT OF OTHERS

Respect is one small word with vast implications. When members of a household or workplace team respect each other and feel respected, relationships run smoothly and interactions occur with ease. Take respect away and people get defensive, despondent, and aggressive.

In the workplace or at home, what each person considers a minimum level of respect may differ, so it is important that acceptably respectful attitudes and behaviours be discussed and agreed upon by all involved.

If, even after negotiation, we feel a lack of respect from someone close to us, it can be tempting to jump straight to domination or coercive work in order to get our way. Some women keep the bottle of Essence of Bend-Over right beside the Love Me and Peaceful Home oils in their supply cupboard. However, although this may be effective in the short term, it is ill-advised over the long haul if you want an equal-exchange partnership or a relationship that doesn't need constant "fixing." In the end, you may get more respect if you offer clear communication and regular expressions of love, even if these may require more effort to manifest.

Here are some herbs that we women can use for winning and holding respect, without interfering with the free will of others.:

HERBS FOR RESPECT
- **Bay Leaf:** The ancient herb woven into crowns of victory keeps your mind clear and causes others to see your natural ability.
- **Black Cohosh Root:** Provides courage and strength when timidity, fear and shyness are getting in the way of being respected.
- **Blood Root:** Helps encourage the respect of blood ties. Useful when children are getting sassy or family members are fighting.
- **Master Root:** To help develop an aura and behaviour which embodies authority and garners respect from others.
- **Rosemary:** When the women of the house aren't being heard, this herb helps give them strength to maintain the upper hand. This power herb for women and mothers can be used liberally in cooking.
- **Sage:** For wisdom; people will look to you for advice.
- **Slippery Elm Bark:** Gossip, slander and lies will slide off of you.
- **Solomon's Seal Root:** Helps you keep your temper and play the part of the wise judge when others lose their tempers.

EMPOWERING YOURSELF WITH CHARISMA

Charisma is the mysterious, elusive ability to attract others in a magnetic manner that inspires devotion, admiration, and love in large numbers of people. At its most negative, charisma is associated with cult leaders, con men, and politicians, but it more properly and benignly describes the personal grace we associate with a well-loved celebrity, a gracious athlete, a dynamic philanthropist, the teacher or coach we loved most at school, the lover we will remember as long as we live.

Charisma is both a mark of divine favour and a matter of how we project ourselves to others. While some people seem to be naturally charismatic — born leaders, fascinating people you meet once and never forget — others have trained themselves in the art. You too can become socially, sexually, and personally charismatic, if it is your will to do so.

SPIRITUAL SUPPLIES FOR CHARISMA
- **Bewitching:** Creates an enchanting "je ne sais quoi" that keeps people coming back for more.
- **Influence:** Helps your words and actions affect the minds of others.
- **Jezebel:** For seductive and daring charisma, the kind associated with "the wild side of life."
- **Look Me Over:** Attracts attention; you can take it from there!

MOJO HAND FOR CHARISMA
Write your desire on a petition paper, put a few of your hairs in it, and fold the the paper towards you. Place it in a red or purple cloth square or drawstring bag along with a large piece of Master Root, a large pinch of Master of the Woods, a large pinch of Deer's Tongue, a few John the Conqueror chips, a few small pieces of Calamus Root, and a small pinch of Black Cohosh Root chips. Feed it weekly with whiskey.

EMPOWERING YOUR PERFUME FOR CHARISMA
No matter what type of perfume you use, you can make it more charismatic, and more identified as your own, by taking the same herbal ingredients given for the mojo hand above, grinding them coarsely and covering them with your perfume in a tightly closed bottle. Steep the mixture for one month, then decant and use the perfume as usual.

ESTABLISHING YOUR FINANCIAL STABILITY

Achieving financial stability means that you will be able to meet all of your basic needs. It is not the same as being rich. Rather, it's about having a reliable income that is budgeted so that your financial goals can be met. It is not living above your means. Rather, it's about saving for unplanned events and setting aside funds to build incrementally for retirement. It's thinking about providing over the long term rather than simply getting things in the short term.

For women, more than for men, long term financial stability can seem like an elusive goal, but by planning ahead, we can Achieve our dreams.

If the pay rates or prospects for promotion are unequal for men and women where we work, we may have to fight for a raise or sharpen our resumés and look for another job. We can do it!

If we fall in love and marry, our long term financial stability may, unfortunately, include keeping some of our money hidden away in case of a break-up or a divorce. If we never have to use it, great — let the money be a gift to our grandchildren!

Remember that in our society, money is time. It's the payment and reward for our time. Now, how do we want to spend our time? How can we get the most value of our time?

We will cease to be afraid to deal with our money if we learn how to make a budget and how to balance a check register. Let us resolve to actively manage our finances and keep our attitude toward money positive. An optimistic approach to dollars and cents will help us move from a world of want to a land of wealth.

Once the mundane aspects of financial stability are addressed, it's time to support our prosperity with spiritual work. What I have noticed about money magic is that working sporadically, only when funds are needed, is far less effective than small but steady on-going work to keep home finances abundant and running smoothly.

MONEY GREENS IN YOUR FOOD

Cooking with dark leafy greens helps draw in money. Collard greens are especially good and can be eaten liberally. Cabbage, Kale, and Spinach work as well. Serve them with beans to add luck and a batch of corn bread with its rich golden colour to craft a full magical meal for financial stability.

HERBS FOR MONEY
- **Alfalfa:** Protects against poverty and prevents financial difficulties.
- **Alkanet Root:** Keeps your money from being jinxed.
- **Allspice:** The whole berries are used in mojos, the powder in foods.
- **Basil:** Grown in the kitchen, it increases wealth and keeps evil away.
- **Cinnamon:** For money-luck, Cinnamon powder is used in cooking, while the chips are carried in mojos or boiled to make scrub water.
- **Fenugreek Seed:** Makes the money you do have last longer.
- **Lodestone:** Attracts money and keeps it. Feed it with Magnetic Sand.
- **Nutmeg:** Carried in a money mojo for luck, also used in cooking.
- **Pyrite:** Sparkly and golden in tone, it is a money attractant.
- **Sassafras:** Dry a Sassafras leaf flat in your wallet for money-luck. Boil the root of the plant to make a money tea-wash for the home.
- **Thyme:** Helps investments grow; for long-term financial planning.

SPIRITUAL SUPPLIES FOR MONEY
- **Boss Fix:** To get a raise, promotion, or better benefits on the job.
- **Money Drawing:** The most popular formula to bring in money, it is employed both in business and in gambling ventures.
- **Money House Blessing:** Helps home finances and those with home-based businesses. Use in scrub water or to dress a lamp in the window.
- **Money Stay With Me:** To help in budgeting, when negotiating to pay less, and to avoid loss through unforeseen circumstances.
- **Pay Me:** To get back pay, settlements, or money that is owed to you.
- **Prosperity:** Improves your attitude toward money, particularly if you feel you don't deserve financial security or think money is unclean.
- **Wealthy Way:** For lifestyle success and true wealth.

AN ABUNDANCE ALTAR IN THE KITCHEN
Making a permanent altar space for money in the home is a well-advised method as it sets up a physical place for money to grow. In the kitchen, above the fridge or on a window-sill are good locations. A small doily, a large Lodestone, and your choice of a potted Basil, Thyme, or Lucky Bamboo plant are all that's needed. Small statues, curios, coins. and photos that symbolize wealth can be added if desired. Actively work the space by burning incense, feeding the Lodestone, watering the plant, burning candles, and adding to or handling the items.

INCENSE FOR WEALTH AND FINANCIAL PROTECTION

Combine equal parts of powdered Dragon's Blood resin, crushed Alkanet Root, and powdered Cinnamon, and burn it as an incense on charcoal to bring in financial prosperity and prevent your money from being jinxed by others. A pinch of this same herb mixture can also be placed in the corners of the room or carried in your wallet, folded into a two-dollar bill on which you've written your name 9 times.

TAKE CARE HOW YOU HANDLE YOUR PURSE

The purse in which you carry your money is more than just a place to carry cash; it is a place where money-magic is generated.

• Never set your purse down on the floor or your money will go down; instead, hold it on your lap, hang it up, or set it in a chair or on a table.

• If you keep an empty purse in your closet without a single coin in it; it will gradually go "dead" and lose its power to draw money to you.

• If you give a purse or a wallet as a gift, it is a friendly gesture to put at least a penny in it so it will be lucky for the recipient.

A SINGLE LODESTONE TO DRAW IN MONEY

Magically, my favourite ways of generating financial stability revolve around ongoing works that are set up and then maintained over time. A large, extra-large or specimen-sized Lodestone is an excellent way to draw and keep money. The magnetism does the attracting while the mass of the stone holds it down. These impressive rocks are also a visual reminder of your financial commitment, and they can be kept going for months or years at a time. Set your Lodestone on a "nest" of paper money and coins and feed it with Magnetic Sand or Anvil Dust until it grows "hairs." Spend the coins, and add more as you wish, to draw more money. When the stone looks dusty, brush off the hairs, wash it in whiskey or Hoyt's Cologne, clean up the feed, and start over.

MONEY LUCK FOR THE HOME

Put a piece of Black Snake Root and a piece of Lodestone grit in a small bottle of Hoyt's Cologne, carry it on your person for three days to that it picks up your essence, and then bury the bottle upright in the ground near your doorstep with a coin placed face-up on top of the cap. You can lightly cover the coin with a leaf, so it will not be seen.

MONEY STAY WITH ME ON YOUR DURABLE GOODS

The importance of keeping your money cannot be over-emphasized. I recommend Money Stay With Me to all of my clients who want increased prosperity in their lives. This is most particularly true in situations where financial difficulties are recurrent, since getting money is only half of the equation — and keeping it is the other half. One way to keep your money is to avoid breakage of expensive equipment. Dress your durable goods, such as the stove, refrigerator, washing machine, vehicle, and tools, with a cross or X of Money StayWith Me oil, or smoke them lightly with Money Stay With Me Incense. Pray the 23rd Psalm as you do this.

LUCKY MONEY BESAMIM SPICES

In *Hoodoo Bible Magic* by Miss Michæle and Professor Porterfield, we learn that "Besamim is a traditional spice mixture used every week by Jews at the Havdalah, a brief ceremony marking the formal conclusion to the Sabbath on Saturday nights. Specific ingredients and their number vary from maker to maker, but besamim is required to be fragrant, for its aroma is inhaled while praying thankfully to God for the creation of the 'varieties of spices.' In hoodoo, besamim has long been marketed as a Lucky Money Herb Mix of Cinnamon, Cloves, Myrtle, Hyssop, Rosemary, Anise, and Bay Leaf. You may inhale the scent, burn the mixture as incense, add it to a bath, dress money with it, or use it to roll candles in, while praying: *'Lord God who made the sweet perfumes, sweeten my money matters.'*"

A DOLLAR BILL FOR A WEALTHY WAY

Here's a spell for fun times, when work is over, as related by Miss cat:

"On the back of a dollar bill, write this verse of Deuteronomy 28:8: *"The Lord shall command the blessing upon thee in thy storehouses, and in all that thou settest thine hand unto; and he shall bless thee in the land which the Lord thy God giveth thee."* On the front write your first and last names. Place it under a plate. Inscribe your name on a green offertory candle and dress it with Wealthy Way Oil. Burn it for a few minutes every evening when you come home from work. Drip oil on the wick each time you light it. After five days of work, you are ready for your weekend, so come home and put five drops of oil on the dollar bill — at the corners and center. Then light the money on fire and burn it to ashes. Rub the ashes on the soles of your shoes, let the candle burn to the socket, go out, and have a good time."

ℙHE ℙOVER

BEGIN BY LOVING AND RESPECTING YOURSELF

There are many ways to love, from married monogamy to dedicated polyamory to wild one-night-stands, but no matter how or whom we love, we will start by loving ourselves, because if we can't love and respect ourselves, it will be difficult or impossible to truly love anybody else.

What if you don't love yourself?

It's a sad fact that many women struggle with feelings of worthlessness and self-hate. We want love, but if we hate ourselves, our "love" is little more than an attachment originating in a place of internal weakness. It has an agenda. It's clingy. There's a fear of loss. The relationship is used as a barometer of personal worth and desirability. This type of "love" is often characterized by jealousy, obsession, and repeated verbal conflicts.

What if you're already in a relationship?

If phrases like "My life would be worthless without him," "I'm nothing without her," and "I'd die if I lost him," have a regular place in your thoughts, you may want to take the time to do some self-love work.

The same applies if you're staying in an abusive relationship or with a toxic partner because you feel you don't deserve better. "Settling" for abuse and disrespect often points to underlying feelings of inadequacy.

If we have suffered years of self-denigration, self-disgust, or self-apathy, how do we turn the tide? How do we embrace ourselves so that we can find the soulmate we seek? Like the child learning to walk, we do it one small step at a time. Therapy, spiritual counselling, and magical work can change how we value ourselves. Begin by nurturing a loving and respectful relationship with your self — going back to the section on personal power for ideas if necessary.

A WOMAN'S LOCKET TALISMAN FOR SELF-LOVE

Get a locket with spaces for two pictures inside. In one, place a picture of yourself, in the other, a loving ancestress. If you have no such ancestress, select a historical female whose spirit will assist you. Ask the ancestress to watch over you, love you, and teach you self-love. Dress the locket regularly with Rose Oil. Touch it at any time you feel weak. You are loved!

A DOLL-BABY FOR SELF LOVE

This spell was suggested by nagasiva yronwode: Create a doll-baby for yourself, choosing a fabric that you find luxurious and beautiful, or a scrap from a worn-out piece of your own clothing that holds good memories for you. Hand-sew the dollie together with red thread that has first been dipped in Love Me Oil. At each stitch say aloud "Loved" or "Cherished." Stuff the dollie with a whole Angelica Root at the head, a small John the Conqueror Root at the heart, and two Balm of Gilead buds at the genitals, filling in around these with your personal concerns, Althæa leaf, Catnip, White Clover flowers, Lavender flowers, Master of the Woods, Forget-Me-Mot flowers, and Spanish Moss or Thistle fluff (the white wings the seeds are scattered by) as a stuffing.

Baptize the doll in your name and talk sweet to it at least once a week, although it is preferable to work it daily. Tell the doll, little you, that it's safe, loved, and cherished. Tell the doll it is respected and cared for. It can also be smoked in incenses such as Love Me, Blessing, Healing, and Bewitching if desired. Wrap the doll in a white handkerchief and keep it in a safe place where others won't be able to harm it: a private drawer works well.

A TOBY FOR SELF-LOVE

On a small piece of paper, write out your wish for authentic and lasting love of yourself. Sign the paper, kiss the paper, and fold it around a Tonka Bean. Sew a heart charm onto a red mojo bag, and inside it place the Tonka Bean packet with Verbena, Elecampane, Mistletoe, and a Southern (Dixie) John Root. Wear it in your bra or against the skin, feeding it weekly with a combination of Crucible of Courage and Dixie John condition oils.

MISS CAT'S "WAKE UP" HAND FOR A WOMAN

"In the center of a square of red flannel cloth place the clippings from all ten of your fingernails, all ten of your toenails, and a hair each from your head, eyebrows, eyelashes, armpits, and pubes. Add a piece of Queen Elizabeth Root, three Coffee beans, and a slice of dried Ginger Root. Pray for your desires, pinch the cloth together to make a ball, and wrap string around it at the "neck" to close it and form a tail. Carry it on you and feed it weekly with a favourite perfume or Crown of Success Oil."

WHEN YOU'RE READY FOR A RELATIONSHIP

If we're comfortable on our own, then we know we're ready for love. Learning to be solitary is an important life skill that helps us maintain a healthy degree of self-identity when we do join in union with another.

Independence and a solid sense of self help us to avoid creating a false front when meeting potential mates. While we'll always put a good foot forward with someone new, we shouldn't feel inauthentic or fraudulent, or hide our true selves when dealing with another person.

True love is generous in nature. When we love someone honestly and whole-heartedly, we aren't lost without them although we miss them. We're still strong and able, even if there's pain. This isn't merely an intellectual exerciseit's a profound understanding from within. Wegive of ourseleves because wecan and want to, not because of the expectation that we'll be getting something back in return for affection.

Don't rush learning to love yourself. Don't think of it as the boring prep-work on the way to the real love work. It is the real love work. Enjoy it, savour it, get excited about it. Once self-love is established, the rest of your love life will begin to come into view.

Now is the time to let the Universe (and your friends) know that you are ready for a relationship. Focus your mind on what you are hoping for and what you can offer to another. Don't select a specific mate yet; just ask for spiritual opportunities to see your prospects clearly.

HERBS FOR KNOWING WHAT YOU REALLY WANT
- **Dittany of Crete:** For assessing what is desired in a future mate.
- **Mint:** Provides mental strength and clarity.
- **Sage:** An aid to thinking and acting from a place of wisdom.
- **Yarrow:** Helps bring courage to look at things honestly.

SPIRITUAL SUPPLIES FOR DECISION-MAKING
- **Clarity:** Brings better understanding of the dynamics of a situation; comprehension of the choices available.
- **Crucible of Courage:** Helps foster the strength necessary to look at choices, people, and situations honestly.
- **King Solomon Wisdom:** For wise decision-making; it also evokes the Song of Solomon, the most beautiful love poem in the Bible.

THREE-DAY SPELL TO OPEN THE ROAD TO LOVE

This three day spell, half-way between a Road Opener and a Love Drawing, breaks dysfunctional patterns from past relationships, releases old hurts, and freshens you to move on to find a new lover.

Begin by preparing two short lists:
- The character traits that you no longer want in a lover.
- The character traits that you want in your next lover.

Dress a red jumbo or pillar candle with Road Opener Oil, and roll it in a mixture of fine-cut Broom, Lemon Balm, and Heart's Ease (Violet) herbs. Set it on a plate over a photo and a personal concern of yourself, plus the list of traits you want in a lover. Place the list of traits you're leaving behind in back of the candle.

Use a good grade of Love Herbs Mixture to draw the outline of a widening road, out in front of and originating from the candle. There should be a small line of herbs on either side of this symbolic pathway.

Steep a tablespoon of Lemon Balm in a cup of hot water for 7 minutes. Strain it and add honey if desired. Light the candle, and in front of it, at the beginning of the road, set a whole Dixie John Root. Sip the tea as you watch the candle flame. Pray for the love you desire and resolve to let go of past losses. Let the candle burn down by a third and pinch it out.

The second day make another cup of Lemon Balm tea and light the candle, this time setting a small heart-shaped stone about half-way down the road. Let the candle burn down by a third and pinch it out.

The third day make a final cup of Lemon Balm tea and light the candle, set a chunk of Myrrh resin at the end of the road, and let the candle burn down to its conclusion.

As the candle nears its end, light the list of qualities you are leaving behind on fire, set it in a fire-proof container with a pinch of finely cut Broom herb, and let it burn to ash. Pass a red flannel bag through the heat of the flame, being careful not to singe or burn it. Add to the bag the roots along the road — the Myrrh, the heart-stone and the Dixie John Root. Add a pinch of the herb mix from either side of the road. Remove the list of traits and personal concerns from below the candle and fold them into a packet around a small Magnet. Add the packet to the bag and breathe your heartfelt prayers for a rewarding love into the toby before tying it shut. Dispose of the spell remains in a crossroads. Keep the mojo and wear it in your bra, feeding it with whiskey weekly.

HOW TO CHOOSE THE RIGHT MATE

When we go to the grocery store without a list, particularly if we're hungry, we usually leave with twice as much food as we actually need, and most of it is not essential to our health. Looking for a lover can go the same way. If we're desperate just to have someone in the bed, chances are that the ones we pick up won't be a good for us over the long haul.

The other extreme, looking for the "ideal" mate with no faults, who magically fixes all of life's problems, is also an endeavour doomed for failure. Pretty much no one lives up to that degree of expectation, particularly after the initial romance ends and reality sets in.

Instead, begin by selecting a spectrum of potentially compatible people with character traits and habits that mesh with your own. Next, decide on what faults you can live with, since no person will ever be perfect. Those who offer a combination of compatibilities and "passable faults" are the ones worth taking the time to get to know. Then define what the deal-breakers are for you. What behaviours, opinions, and actions are not open to negotiation? What will cause you to end a relationship with no hope of reconciliation? Once you are sure what you want, then work can begin in a targeted and deliberate manner to attract that kind of person, increasing chances of a successful outcome.

LOVE-DIVINATION CANDLES ROLLED IN LOVE-HERBS

Deacon Millett of FourAltars.com tells how to prepare herb-rolled love light candles: "To roll freestanding candles in herbs, just barely melt a layer of wax on a cookie sheet over a stove or in an oven. Don't let it get too hot. Sprinkle on finely crushed love herbs like Catnip, Dill, shredded Rose petals, Damiana, Violet, Spikenard, Elecampane, Patchouli, or Verbena, to which you have added a few drops of Love Me, Return To Me, or Reconciliation Oil. Remove the cookie-sheet from the heat and as the wax begins to harden, roll the candles in it to coat them. The result may look lumpy and 'organic.' Don't worry; that's normal."

To choose among several prospects, name one candle for each person, roll all the candles in love herbs, light them all at once, watch as they burn, and read the remnant wax for signs of love, indifference, or problems.

For detailed instructions on how to read candle wax, see: LuckyMojo.com/candlemagicdivination.html by Cat Yronwode

LOVING, AS YOU LIKE IT

Now we will explore some options for dating, romance, love, and sex. If your beliefs include the preservation of virginity until marriage, save the rest of this chapter to read only after you have wed.

If you want to "test the waters" before setting sail on the sea of matrimony, by all means, learn what you can here, and do practice safe sex and birth control until you are sure of your partner's history and intentions.

What kind of person makes your heart sing? What's really important for you in a mate? Do you need a talker? A doer? A laugher? A sex-god? A moneymaker? Someone who can screw in a light bulb?

Next consider what kind of a relationship you're looking for. Do you do better with long-term partners? Are you a serial monogamist? Perhaps a swinger? Is polyamory a better fit for you? Do you want someonestable at home with an occasional affair on the side? There's space for all of these in the socio-sexual repertoire of modern society, particularly if you recognize and are honest about what you want.

Finally, consider compatibility. What makes or breaks a marriage may not be how much you love each other or how closely uour lifestyles match, but differences in your degree of neatness or talkativeness. The Devil's in the details and they're what can drive you bananas twenty years down the line, once you no longer see your partner through rose-tinted glasses.

Put all this information together and it will provide a profile of many potentially great partners to choose from. One you have set your sights on them the next step is to draw them to you, singly or serially, as you choose.

DRESSING YOUR BED TO DRAW PROSPECTIVE MATES

Think of the space you inhabit as a Spider's web. The outer rows of web are your city, neighbourhood, and the block you live on. The inner rows are your yard, the outer and inner perimeters of your house, your bedroom corners, and the corners of your bed. Using a map, trace a route that spirals in toward your bed, large enough to be seen by the angels, not so long that it cannot be walked. Mark the perimeter with love oils and your personal essences. Follow your path inward, marking every turn, and asking your true love to follow the scent to your bed. Conclude with the corners of the house, the corners of the bedroom, and the corners of the bed, then place yourself at the center of the bed and declare, "Here I am, come to me!"

RED CANDLE AND LODESTONE LOVE-DRAWING SPELL

This is my variation on a 7-day spell which Catherine Yronwode suggests for bringing around a new lover, whether known or unknown. On the first day, rise before the Sun does and draw a warm bath. Dissolve half a pack each of Lodestone and Come To Me Bath Crystals in the water. Bathe upward from feet to head, while thinking of the love you want to draw in. Save a sample of the used water before getting out of the tub and letting yourself air dry. Dress in fresh clothes and oil yourself with a love oil such as Come To Me, Lavender Love Drops, or Dixie Love. As the Sun rises, sprinkle the remnant bath water on the sidewalk and path leading up to your home, and in through the door.

Fit a matched pair of Lodestones together, then separate and set them at either edge of a plate. Name one for yourself and one for your future lover, calling them by name or office: "You are now my future mate, and my future mate shall you always be." Dress them with the love oil and your sexual fluids. Place personal concerns (or a list of traits) below each.

Dress a red figural candle (bride-and-groom, penis, vulva, 7-knob, or lovers) with the oil. Set the candle on a fire-safe surface directly behind the plate, forming a triangle of the two stones and the candle. Place an incense burner behind the candle, also on a fire-proof surface. Light a love-drawing incense like Come To Me, Lavender Love Drops or Dixie Love and then light the candle. Feed each Lodestone with Magnetic Sand, as you speak your desire aloud or read passages from the Song of Solomon. Let the candle burn one-seventh of the way down and snuff it out.

The next day, light some incense and the candle once more. Move the Lodestones closer together and feed them again with Magnetic Sand. Repeat the prayers and optional Bible readings. Let the candle burn one-seventh of the way down and snuff it out.

Repeat the incense burning, candle burning and Lodestone moving and feeding every day. On the seventh day the candle should burn out, the Lodestones should be touching and well-covered with Magnetic Sand.

When the work is complete, place the two Lodestones on their plate in a safe place, where they will continue to attract one another, such as under your bed. Leftover incense ash and wax can be wrapped in a piece of red flannel, tied with red thread, and buried beneath your front steps, in a flowerbed or garden, or in a potted plant – a maidenhair fern if you can get one. Then take a final sunrise bath with the other half of the bath crystals.

AN OLD-FASHIONED HAT TRICK

Miss Cat says, "If a woman loves a man more than he loves her, she can ask to wear his hat, either in playfulness or because of the weather. Once she has his hat, she should pretend that she needs to go to the bathroom. While out of sight, she should pull down her pants and rub the hat between her legs. After that, she should give the hat back, and he will love her more."

LOVE POTION NO. 9: A GLAMOUR SPELL TO DRINK

This recipe comes from the wonderful teaching team of Madame Nadia and Madame Pamita. "Mix these nine edible love herbs in a muslin bag. As you put each herb in the bag, ask it to do your love work: Cardamom Seeds, Cinnamon Stick, Coriander Seeds, Damiana, Ginger, Lovage Root, Peppermint, Red Clover, and Red Rose petals.

"Soak the bag in wine or brandy for nine days, remove the bag and use the liquid as a tincture. Alternatively, steep the bag in boiled water for nine minutes to make a tea, and add honey or sugar. Serve to your lover while gazing into his or her eyes."

The addition of a drop of your menstrual blood or sexual fluids before serving the drink will mark it as yours, making it more specific in intent.

A WOMAN'S MOJO TO DRAW A MATE FOR LOVE

Here's a mojo from Miss cat: "To make this little hand you will need the hair of the man you want. Pubic hair is best, but other hairs will do. Prepare a 3″ square name-paper using red ink to write the man's name over and over in a spiral leading to the center of the paper, where you will draw a heart. Touch the heart with your sexual fluids. Use menstrual blood if you have it available; if it is gooey enough, stick the man's hair right in it.

"Fold the paper by the corners-in method, so that each corner is brought to the middle, and the newly created corners are also brought to the middle. Seal it with sticky red wax, tape, or glue. Dress the paper with Follow Me Boy Oil. Place it in a square of red flannel with a piece of Queen Elizabeth Root, two Red Rose buds, two Lodestone grits, Lavender flowers, Spikenard, and other love curios, and sew the flannel into a packet small enough to wear on your person. Let your sweat get on it, then dress it with your own favourite perfume. If you wear it in your bosom, you will charm the man you desire with your special winning ways.

"For female same-sex love, use Q Oil or Follow Me Girl Oil."

MISS CAT'S FOLLOW ME BOY BATH SPELL

"Follow Me Boy is a conjure formula for dressing oil, incense, sachet powders, and bath products that enable a woman to dominate and control a man. The ingredients include Catnip, Damiana, and Calamus Root, plus other herbs and essences. Here is a typical Follow Me Boy bath ritual of the type that has been popular since the 1910s.

"Empty half a packet of Follow Me Boy Bath Crystals into a basin of hot water to dissolve them. Float red flower petals in the water.

"Standing in your tub or shower stall, pour the prepared water over your head as you say, '[Name of lover], follow me,' and bathe thoroughly, but only by rubbing your body upward (not downward). If you don't want to wet your hair, pour from the face and neck only. Dry yourself and collect the used bath water, which now has your essence in it. Dress in fresh, clean, red clothes, with red and golden jewelry.

"Make some Follow Me Boy Incense up into cones or place it loose on a brazier. Lay down lines of the Follow Me Boy Sachet Powder on your altar in the form of a six-pointed star made of two triangles, upward-pointing for the man, downward-pointing for yourself. Put the man's photo in the center of the star. Place candle holders at the six points. Carve the full name of the man on each of six red candles and dress them with Follow Me Boy Oil, rubbing them in the palm of your hand to anoint them in exactly the same way and with the same attention you would stroke your lover. As each candle is dressed, place it at one of the six points of the star, setting out his triangle first, and then yours. Concentrate on your desires and say out loud '[Name of lover], follow me. [Name of lover], come under my command.' Let the candles burn until they go out.

"Go to the man's house and throw your remnant bath water and some of the flower petals on his doorstep or in his yard, saving some to mark the path back to your house, sprinkling water and flowers at each crossroads you pass along the way back to your place and on your own doorstep. At each stop, say out loud '[Name of lover], follow me. [Name of lover], come under my command.' If stopping on the way is inconvenient for you, sprinkle all the remaining water and flowers on your own doorstep. If he lives too far to go to his house, write him a letter on paper sprinkled with your bath water and dried, then sprinkled with some saved sachet powder. Enclose one of the red flower petals. He will come to you and follow you like a dog."

OUR SECRET: MENSTRUAL BLOOD MAGIC

All across the world in a dizzying cross-section of magical practices, vaginal secretions have been used in love spells — and of all of these secretions, menstrual blood reigns supreme. Archæologists theorize that in ancient Mesopotamia, conception charms were made from clay dolls smeared with menstrual blood. In ancient Egypt, menstrual blood was said have protective virtues, and according to other traditions, when mixed with red wine and ingested, it was thought to increase spiritual power. The fluid is used as an ingredient in European philters and love potions, and it is directly fed to lovers in Sicilian folk magic as well as in conjure. In other cultures it has been mixed with fertilizers or simply spread on fields to ensure their fertility.

Throughout the world, period blood has been seen as a potent force of generation and creation. It was long believed that menstrual blood, not the ovum, was the alma mater of the human form, the blood of life from which we are created. According to this theory, menstrual blood coagulated and made physical the soul within the womb. Although the mechanics of procreation have since been clarified by the lens of science, the single quintessentially female right and privilege still remains the ability to make life. Menstrual blood is a powerful reminder of our capacity to create life or magic — which is why venous or arterial blood cannot replace it in spells.

In keeping with society's numerous other forms of female body-shaming, it comes as no surprise that quite a few men and women consider menstruation to be at worst "unclean" and at best a "nuisance." We have been supplied with modern medicines to mask cramping, taught to use tampons and pads to hide and dispose of the evidence, and even offered hormonal treatments to trick the body out of its monthly blood. Despite this, many among us purposefully reclaim our "Moon time" as a period of power, command, or introspection during which we can reconnect to our own needs and truths as women.

If you enjoy your menstrual period, including the expulsive cramps and liquid flows, you can spiritually elevate both the event and its significance, but even if it hurts, you can still learn to work with the potent force of your monthly blood for your own benefit, in realms of experience as diverse as romance, attraction, seduction, sexuality, territory marking, controlling, binding, coercion, and marital fidelity.

COLLECTING MENSTRUAL BLOOD

Methods for collecting menstrual blood vary depending on the type of feminine hygiene products used.

- **Disposable Sanitary Napkins:** If you use disposable pads, cut out the section bearing blood and let it dry. Remove any "dry-weave" type barrier on the top or adhesive backing layer. The pad's blood can be included as your personal concern in love spells. Pads can also be rehydrated with water and the liquid added to beverages or foods.

- **Washable Sanitary Napkins:** When dealing with washable napkins, soak the soiled pad in a small volume of water prior to washing in order to release the blood. This water can be evaporated to leave the blood residue or it may be used as-is.

- **Tampons:** Dry and store tampons for future use. Their shape makes them great "tea bags" for dosing drinks or foods. A swish or two through the liquid is good enough for some folks, but others let it stew a while. Tampons can be cut into sections once dry, thereby stretching their use over time. Be aware, however, that storing dried tampons is far from discreet if someone finds them, and, worse, if your tampon is found, an enemy can use it against you by boring a hole in a tree and driving the tampon in with a wooden peg to stop up your blood.

- **Menstrual Cups:** As the blood is collected, it can be poured directly into a cup, jar, or other container; there is no medium from which the blood needs to be extracted. This method yields the greatest volume of liquid for those who intend to use menstrual blood for crop fertility.

- **Morning Cup Collection:** If a pad is worn overnight, blood will accumulate in the vagina and in the morning upon waking your flow will be heavier. When you first get up to pee in the morning, place a cup beneath the vagina and catch the overflow, using a few Kegel exercises to help push the accumulated fluid out.

- **Swab Collection:** You can always use Q-Tips to swab some blood when your monthly flow is heaviest. These can be bagged and frozen to use later. They have the advantage of being smaller and more portable than dried tampons or disposable pads.

- **Finger Collection:** Not too many women like to admit it, but if you are in the kitchen cooking, it's easiest of all to stick your finger in and get what you need, then dip your finger in the sauce.

PRESERVING MENSTRUAL BLOOD

Because menstrual blood is proteinaceous, it will spoil or "go bad" if not properly preserved.

- **Fresh Menstrual Blood:** Use it at once, on the day it is collected.
- **Refrigerated Liquid Blood:** Refrigerated blood will keep for several days. Some women add a dash of high-proof whiskey, vodka, or gin, to the blood for preservation purposes, but this is not really necessary.
- **Frozen Blood:** Make ice-cubes using a freezer tray. To each section add a few drops of liquid menstrual blood and mix well. There should be very little discolouration of the water. Frozen blood will last almost indefinitely, and will eventually dry up as the ice sublimates.
- **Dried Blood:** Aluminum foil smeared with blood and set in a warm place will dry quickly. By bending the foil, the dried solids will flake off. The flakes can then be ground to a fine powder and easily added to spices, sprinkled over food, or blended into sachet powders.

SNEAKY WAYS TO FEED MENSTRUAL BLOOD FOR LOVE

Feeding someone your period blood for love-drawing is often done as a "sneaky" trick. Some of the most usual methods include:

- **Menstrual Blood Ice-Cubes:** Freeze and add to beverages, sauces, or foods being prepared for the person.
- **Beverages:** Reddish liquids such as Hibiscus tea, fruit punch, berry juice, fruit soda, or wine hide blood perefectly, and dark liquids like coffee, tea, cola, and whiskey are also well-suited to being dosed.
- **Foods:** Reddish, brownish, and dark are the keys to adding menstrual blood to food. Spaghetti sauce, chili, ketchup, chocolate, mollases, or spiced baked goods are traditional choices.
- **Kiss and Don't Tell:** Go to the bathroom, get some blood on your finger, smear it on your lips, and camouflage it with lipstick. Come out of the washroom, kiss the person open-mouthed, and use your tongue to introduce some of the fluid into his or her mouth.
- **Oral Sex:** At the very end or beginning of your menstrual cycle, when the flow is barely perceptible, have your partner go down on you: he'll dose himself that way. Note that some men will not perform oral sex at all, for fear of being tricked in this manner.

A WORD OF MEDICAL CAUTION WHEN FEEDING BLOOD

If you plan to feed period blood to a man, be sure that you are not carrying a sexually transmitted or blood-borne disease that may be transmitted by ingestion. If you do carry such an illness, limit your use of blood to drawing sigils, and dressing curios, candles, and talismans.

FEEDING MENSTRUAL BLOOD TO A MAN TO BIND HIM

The best known magical use for menstrual blood is to feed it to a male lover to catch him, capture him, bind him, or cause him to stay with you,

Binding a man does not always mean that he will be faithful or that he can't break up with you, nor does it make him your slave. However, once caught, if he wishes to leave, he will have to make an effort to break free. He can do this for himself or hire a root doctor to take your work off of him.

Repeated doses may be needed to bind a resistant man, but unless he is protected, he needs only be fed your blood one time to be bound. Still, many women feed their men at every period as "maintenance" work.

When feeding menstrual blood to a man, just add it to his food or drink and pray your desire; the blood itself does the work. Some people believe that accidental ingestion of a woman's period blood, such as might occur within the context of oral sex, can result in binding, even without the woman's intention. In my own experience I have found this to be true.

BINDING A MAN VERSUS TYING HIS NATURE

What men fear most is not being bound; it is having their nature tied so that they can't get hard or have an orgasm with any woman other than the one who hoodooed them. There are many ways to tie a man's nature, but although most employ a knot spell made with the man's semen and the measure of his erect penis, men who are afraid of having their nature tied tend to believe that if they avoid tasting menstrual blood, their nature will remain free. Their pointed avoidance of "red sauce" makes them difficult to bind, and, ironically, leaves them vulnerable to having their nature tied.

Of course, if you are serious about capturing a man, you will both bind him with your blood and tie his nature with his semen on a knotted string. See page 73 for details.

If you meet a man whose nature was tied by another woman, you should know how to break that off of him so you can enjoy his company, See page 95 for details.

THERE IS POWER IN THE BLOOD

From 1936 to 1940, the Reverend Harry Middleton Hyatt collected hoodoo, conjure, and rootwork spells from black practitioners throughout the South. Here are a few women's uses for menstrual blood:

MENSTRUAL BLOOD TO KEEP YOUR MAN ASLEEP

In 1936 a woman in Ocean City, Maryland, said that if you take "a lady's difficulty" and put it under a man's nose while he sleeps, he won't wake up until she removes it, and "she can get his money and do anything."

In 1938 a woman in Brunswick, Georgia, told Hyatt that if you hide your soiled menstrual pad under the mattress, then lightly throw your nightgown over your man's face while he is asleep, you can go out all night long and he will not wake up until you come home in the morning.

SEX WORKER'S SPELL TO KEEP A MAN COMING BACK

In 1937, a worker in Savannah, Georgia, told Rev. Hyatt that if a man who sells liquor wants to fix a male customer to return frequently, he will get the man's fingernails or toenails and scorch them, add money spices like Cinnamon, Allspice, Cloves, Nutmeg, and Mace, and carry the mix in a little bag. But if a prostitute wants a male customer to return frequently, she will instead put the man's scorched nails and the spices in whiskey, add her "discharge," strain it, and give it to the man to drink.

MENSTRUAL BLOOD TO STOP A MAN FROM DRINKING

In 1938 a woman in Memphis, Tennessee, told how to sicken a man so that he would quit drinking. On the third day of your period, you should collect three drops of menses and put it in whiskey. On the fourth day of your period, collect four more drops and add them to the whiskey. Put two needles into the whiskey bottle, and shake it well, saying, "I'm putting this here to stick you in your whiskey drinking, to stop you from drinking." Remove the needles and serve him the whiskey and it will make him sick.

PRESERVING (AND SERVING) MENSES FOR LOVE

In 1939, a practitioner in Savannah, Georgia, told Rev. Hyatt that women take nine drops of menstrual blood, put it into whiskey as a preservative, and when their sweethearts come to visit, they serve whiskey out of that bottle to draw love to themselves.

MENSTRUAL BLOOD AND HIS LETTER FOR REUNION

In 1939 in Fayetteville, North Carolina, a woman explained how to get a man to return home: If he writes you a letter, cut the four corners off of it to make a diamond shape. Put some menstrual blood on a small square of red flannel and place it in the middle of the cut letter, then fold one of the newly-made corners to the opposite corner, to make a triangle. Repeat this to make a smaller triangle, and again to make a very small triangle. After it is folded, wear it in your underwear, in contact with your genitals.

MENSTRUAL BLOOD IN ALTAR WORK

In addition to the use of menstrual blood in food or drink or by direct contact, here is an array of ways that it can be used in altar work:

- **Anointing:** Lodestones, Queen Elizabeth Roots, and Cowrie shells can be dressed with menstrual blood as a personal concern when working love spells. Candles can also be fixed with menstrual blood, usually within the context of love drawing, female domination, fidelity, or endeavours of personal empowerment.
- **Condition Oil:** Love drawing, love domination, and love fidelity oils such as Stay With Me, Bewitching, I Dominate My Man, Love Me, Come To Me, Kiss Me Now! and Follow Me Boy can be fixed with your powdered menstrual blood to mark the oil as yours. Just make sure you always use the fixed oil on the person you care for, and not in work that you might be doing on someone else's behalf!
- **Petition Papers:** Using menstrual blood as ink or mixing it into red ink to make it easier flowing, write your love petition on paper and set it beneath a candle or put it in a container spell. Alternatively, write the petition on a white plate which you can employ as a candle stand and then wash clean at the conclusion of the work.
- **Container Spells:** A bit of powdered menstrual blood or a piece of dried blood on a menstrual pad can be folded into a petition paper and added to a honey jar, sugar bowl, doll-baby, or mojo bag as a personal concern.
- **Incense:** A bit of powdered menstrual blood can be added to any incense blends used in love work, particularly if the person you love will be exposed to the smoke. Menstrual blood is also an ingredient in the wonderful empowering incense blend on page 33.

FOR THE WOMAN WHO DOES NOT BLEED

Although working with menstrual blood is the most famous of female conjure tricks, many women do not have periods. You may not have regular cycles if you are below the age of puberty, are overweight, are malnourished, engage in extreme exercise, have polycystic ovarian syndrome, are pregnant or nursing, are using a hormone-disruptor form of birth control, are taking certain antipsychotic or antidepressant medications, are undergoing chemotherapy treatment, have a pituitary or thyroid tumour, are using high blood pressure medicines, have had a hysterectomy or oophorectomy, are post-menopausal, or are a transwoman.

When menstrual blood is not available, you may quite satisfactorily substitute vaginal secretions, urine, or sweat from the pubic region.

STRAINING FOOD THROUGH PANTYHOSE

If you do not menstruate, you may feed your lover your essences by wearing thin panties or pantyhose without underwear, and then straining liquids such as water or the liquid from canned tomatoes through the hose.

RUBBING BOTTLED OR CANNED DRINKS ON THE VULVA

If you wish to attract a person sexually, but you will only have contact with a drink via a closed can or bottle, rub the container between your legs and against your vulva to get your scent and fluid on it. This will affect the person when the beverale is opened and consumed.

DEPLOYING VAGINAL SCENT

Vaginal secretions are intimate personal concerns used to attract or bind a lover. They are a link to the self, just as a hair or fingernail is, and they are laden with pheromones, strong animal "perfumes" we subconsciously respond to. Think about your child's smell, or the warm feeling from a lover's scent while you embrace; those are pheromones at work and their non-verbal language of bonding is potent. Pheromones affect the limbic system of the brain, which contributes in the control of sex drive, pleasure, and affection. This is where science and magic meet: science explaining today how magic has been using our noses for millennia.

To deploy vaginal secretions, just dab them behind your ears, with or without the addition of a commercial perfume or spiritual scent.

SINGLE LADIES: PUT A RING ON IT

For most women (although by no means all), falling in love is the beginning of a beautiful path that leads to matrimony. If you have chosen an appropriate mate — one who is mentally sound, single and free to marry, has not been cursed to a life of loneliness, and who does not bear the burdens of alcoholism or addiction — that path may be short, sweet, and even. However, sometimes the one you love is what is called "rough timber," a person who needs a bit of finishing before you can build a home together. And, truth to tell, you may also need to work on your own issues of trust, temperament, and patience.

Start your journey to marriage by deciding how long is too long to get some serious settling-down action happening, and then stick to that time frame. Don't be one of those women who realizes, ten years into a dating or live-in situation, that the one you love will never marry.

Next, do the mundane work to get what you want. Be sweet, show your best side, and play fair with your lover. Let commitment blossom and grow without nipping it in the bud by pushing too hard, insisting on an engagement too soon, or demanding long conversations on "how things are going." Likewise, do not delay or play hard to get out of a sense of dominance or to tease a sincere lover. That first proposal of marriage may not come a second time if you said, "Let's wait," instead of "Yes."

Growing a bond isn't only about working magic; it's about living, loving and sharing in real life. That said, there are many spells to draw a marriage. Try any or all; they will not "cancel each other out."

DRESSING A TEA LIGHT CANDLE FOR MARRIAGE

Get a white tea light that comes in an aluminum cup, plus two tiny Lodestone grits, a pinch of Magnetic Sand, a pinch of Deer's Tongue herb, and Marriage Oil. Pop the candle out of its cup, rub the inside of the cup with the oil, then use a ballpoint pen to inscribe your initials plus the initials of your lover inside a heart. Put the paired Lodestones grits in the center of the cup and feed them with Magnetic Sand. Carve the same heart-and-initials design on the flat top of the candle, put it back in the cup, dress it with the oil, sprinkle the Deer's Tongue on it, and light it. After it has finished, bury the cup with the Lodestones and all still in it, in your yard. Do this weekly, until the house is surrounded and you get your proposal.

MOJO HAND FOR MARRIAGE

Sew a heart charm onto a red flannel bag. Fill it with a pair of Lodestone grits, Magnetic Sand, a Dixie John Root, Red Clover, and a petition for marriage folded around a personal concern from each of you. Wear the toby in your bra or against your skin, feeding it weekly with Marriage Oil or Hoyt's Cologne. On a Monday during each Waxing Moon, place it under a bowl and burn a small candle on top. Work it this way until you are married.

MOJO FOR MARRIAGE AFTER A CUT AND CLEAR SPELL

To break off a bad relationship, do a Cut and Clear spell, like the one at: **LuckyMojo.com/CutandClear.html**

This leaves you with a list of "good traits" desired in your next mate. You can save the list in your underwear drawer or use it to make this mojo:

Sew a heart charm onto a pink bag and place into it a Queen Elizabeth Root, a Dixie John Root, Spikenard, and your personal concerns folded into the list from the Cut and Clear spell, Smoke the bag in Marriage Incense while praying from the Song of Solomon. Wear it in your bra or against the skin, feeding it with Marriage Oil and Dixie John Root In Oil every week.

HONEY OR SUGAR JAR FOR A PROPOSAL

Fill a small jar that has a metal lid with honey or sugar. Write a petition for a proposal of marriage. Make it square, so you can fold it into a seed-packet, as described in *Paper In My Shoe* by Cat Yronwode. Into the packet, put a pair of Lodestone grits and small pieces of Tonka Bean, Spikenard, Deer's Tongue herb, Sandalwood, Frankincense, Solomon's Seal Root, and a personal concern of each of you. Fold and seal the packet, and push it into the sugar or honey, then lick your fingers and say, "As this sugar [or honey] is sweet to me, so will [Name] be sweet to me and agree to a marriage." Some women repeat the prayer three times. Close the jar. You may burn a red or pink candle dressed with Marriage Oil on the lid on Mondays, Wednesdays, and Fridays and / or use the sweetener to cook for your lover, refilling the jar with sugar or honey as the contents get low.

FOR A LONG MARRIAGE

Miss Cat says, "Just as Bay Laurel wreaths were worn by victorious athletes and soldiers in ancient Rome, so it is said that a bit of Laurel in a bride's wreath or bouquet will ensure a long, successful marriage."

THE WIFE

IN MARRIAGE, COMMUNICATION COMES FIRST

Congratulations on your marriage. Now let's see how we can keep it happy and long-lasting. We'll start with the basics of good communication. Clear and respectful communication is essential when people live together. Face to face speech, augmented when necessary by texting, telephoning, or Skyping, fosters closeness and connection and helps a married couple get along. Speech allows us to clarify our wants and needs and settle disagreements. Gentle touch is important, but don't assume that your spouse can read your mind or your body language: Say what you're thinking. Like I tell my two year old: "Use your words!"

Certain skills can be learned to help communicate more effectively. These include active listening; reducing sarcasm; thoughtfully choosing words, tone, and body language; and controlling the level of impulsivity you display when engaged in emotionally difficult exchanges. Many books, courses, and seminars are available which cover these tactics in depth.

HERBS THAT ENHANCE MARITAL COMMUNICATION
- **Borage:** For calm, equanimity, and peace in family relationships.
- **Deer's Tongue:** Helps finds the right words to say something. Good when there are difficult or delicate matters to discuss.
- **Lavender:** To encourage harmony and cooperation, also to help calm situations down.
- **Rosemary:** Gives women rulership and agency within their homes.
- **Tobacco:** Used to carry messages to the minds of those far away.
- **Yarrow:** For courage during times of difficulty. Mix with Deer's Tongue and Rosemary to address problem situations in the home.

SPIRITUAL SUPPLIES FOR MARITAL COMMUNICATION
- **Clarity:** When the issue being discussed isn't clear or when thoughts are clouded, this is the formula to turn to.
- **Crucible of Courage:** Fosters the strength necessary to begin a conversation when a subject is particularly sensitive or hurtful.
- **Mercury:** Improve matters related to communication of any sort.

A BOTTLE SPELL FOR EFFECTIVE COMMUNICATION

Mix together enough Lavender, Sage, and Deer's Tongue to fill a small jar 7/8 of the way to the top while praying Ephesians 4:29 (*"Let no corrupting talk come out of your mouths, but only such as is good for building up, as fits the occasion, that it may give grace to those who hear."*) Light Benzoin resin and Peaceful Home Incense on charcoal.

Prepare a small name paper for each household member. Cross and cover each name with "open and constructive discussion" or "effective communication." Roll each paper, with a hair from that person, into a tight cylinder, rolling toward you. Tie each roll with a piece of thread and five knots. Use small papers and make tight rolls – they need to neatly fit into the jar. Smoke each roll in incense and bury it in the herbs in the jar.

Cover over the herbs with a thick layer of sugar to finish filling the jar. Dress a white candle with a combination of Mercury Oil and Peaceful Home Oil and burn it on the jar weekly, on Mondays. Inscribe the candle with the verse from Ephesians 4:29 before anointing it. Peaceful Home Incense and Benzoin resin may be burned each Monday if so desired.

DOUBLE-DRESSED CANDLE TO RESOLVE A FIGHT

Inscribe a 9" blue candle with your desire for a successful resolution to the fight, as if it has occurred already. Use phrasing like, "[Name] and I respect each other's point of view" or "[Name] and I are in agreement about how to spend the family's spare income." Set aside.

Line a baking pan with foil. Break a 4" white candle into small pieces. (Wrap it in a paper bag first to reduce any mess.) Mix powdered Cloves, Flax seed, a drop of Healing Oil, and the wax in the pan. Melt the mix over a burner at low heat until it is workable and then roll the blue candle in it to cover its surface. Let it harden. The result will be bumpy; that's okay.

Inscribe a 4" black candle. Write all your pain, annoyance, and anger onto it; everything you want to say but haven't, everything that's upsetting you. It doesn't matter if you cover the same area multiple times. Write until you're out of steam. Light the black candle and drip all of its wax over the herb-rolled candle to cover all of the white wax and herbs. No more white should show. Anoint the double-dressed candle with Block Buster Oil.

Dress the name papers with Healing Oil. Place them, name-sides facing one another, with personal concerns between, under a metal plate. Set the candle on the plate and light it. Bury the spell remnants beneath a tree.

WOMEN'S SPIRITUAL COOKING SECRETS

Not every married woman cooks for her mate, but if you do, here are some secrets that every good conjure wife should know:

• **Add Personal Concerns to the Food or Drink:** Bath water with your essence in it, menstrual blood, sexual fluids, urine, and sweat are the most commonly used personal concerns in the preparation of food. They work well in love, fidelity, and domination work. Tears can be added to salt the food if you are asking for forgiveness.

• **Add a Petition to the Food or Drink:** Burn a petition paper to ash, and add a small amount of the ash to food. More subtly, write a petition or Psalm with water-soluble ink on paper or on a white plate, then dissolve the paper prayer or wipe the plate off into food or drink.

• **Use Herbs or Roots with a Specific Purpose:** When ingredients are used for their magical attributes rather than for their taste, they are often hand-ground in a mortar and pestle and prepared with prayer. The ingredients can be used to bake, cook, or tinctured in alcohol.

• **Use Ongoing Spell-Work as an Ingredient:** The honey or sugar from a sweet jar, or the vinegar from a souring spell, can be used in a recipe to affect the person whose name is called into the food.

• **Add Vermin to Food or Drink:** Ground up reptiles, snails, insects, or spiders can be added to food to do grievous harm. This is the basis for a variety of traditional spells that cause "Live Things In You."

• **Make Lucky Foods:** Prepare traditional spiritual foods like black-eyed peas and greens on New Year's for luck and money. Burn red onion skins on the stove for house-luck any time you cook with them.

• **Watch the Handling of Cutlery While Cooking:** To chop up food in a pot with a knife means a dispute in the house; if a knife falls, a man will visit; if a fork falls, a woman will visit; if a spoon falls, a baby will visit; if a girl who is engaged accidentally lets a knife fall, her lover is coming; and handing a person a knife point-first "cuts" your friendship.

• **Put Unwanted People "On Ice":** Way in the back of your freezer is where to keep a special packet of frozen personal concerns and get-away herbs to freeze rivals or unpleasant relatives out of your home.

For fully detailed unstructions on freezer spells, see:
LuckyMojo.com/freezer.html by Catherine Yronwode

HOODOO FOOD!

The recipes on this page are just a taste of the magical cooking ideas to be found in the hook *Hoodoo Food! The Best of the Conjure Cook-Off and Rootwork Recipe Round-Up,* edited by Sister Robin Petersen.

VALENTINE PEAR SALAD

1 can Bartlett Pear halves in juice (love and fertility)
¼ cup Cinnamon Red Hots candies, to taste (fiery love)
Red food colouring (love and passion)

Pour Pear liquid into a small saucepan and add Red Hots. Simmer until candies dissolve, stirring to prevent scorching, then remove from heat. Stir in a drop of food colouring, then add pears, gently, so as not to break them. Spoon sauce over pears repeatedly. When cool, place in refrigerator. Serve on lettuce as a salad or on vanilla ice cream. Valentine Pears are a form of Red Fast Luck.

— Catherine Yronwode, ReadersAndRootworkers.org

THE SECRET LANGUAGE OF CHOCOLATE FILLINGS

Vanilla, the scent of pure love and sexual attraction: "I want you!"
Ginger, for spicing up a love affair: "I'm hot for you!"
Cherry, first love, sexual love, female blood magic: "You are mine!"
Nuts, for male sexuality and virile power: "My man!"
Orange, the flower used in wedding wreaths: "Marry me!"
Maple, a natural sweetener: "Won't you be kind to me?"
Raspberry, faithful and passionate love: "Let's stay home tonight!"

— Pamela Wells, Santa Monica, Calif.

FIRST LOVE CHERRY TOMATOES

12 Cherry Tomatoes cut in half crosswise (women's stuff)
1 8-ounce ærosol can of bacon-cheese spread (men's stuff)
1 tablespoon chopped fresh Dill (to draw love)

Squeeze the seeds and juice out of the Tomatoes, pipe in bacon-cheese spread, and top with dill. A woman is a "Tomato." A virgin has her "cherry." A man's stuff is "bacon and cheese." Putting the bacon in the cherry Tomato with Dill means to get laid for the first time with love. Add period blood if you dare! Serve as an "appetizer." LOL!

— Anonymous (It worked for me!)

HOW TO KEEP A HOME SPIRITUALLY CLEAN

"Cleanliness is next to godliness," but there is no single definition of what "clean" is. It doesn't necessarily mean that the home is spotless with no dish out of place and not a speck of dirt. Rather, "clean" is the level of tidiness at which you feel comfortable, your mind feels uncluttered upon walking in, and you can find what you want, when you want it. A clean home is free of negative energy and spiritual messes. Evil spirits, crossed conditions, and curses on the marriage find no foothold in such a home.

- **Clean in a Pattern and Seal Each Room:** Clean your house from back to front and clean each room from top to bottom. Throw used scrub water outdoors to the West, if possible. Set a small candle or incense in each finished room to seal its goodness in.
- **Add Spiritual Supplies to Household Cleaners:** A capful of Chinese Wash added to mop or laundry water keeps evil away and leaves things refreshed. House Blessing Oil or Peace Water also transmit a positive vibration to the home when added to household cleaners.
- **Add Herb Teas to Scrub Water:** Rue, Basil, Lemongrass, and Pine are excellent herbs for cleansing the home spiritually.
- **Burn Incense to Clear the Air:** After a fight or a negative event, burn Frankincense, Sweet Grass, Pine, Sage, or Palo Santo, or use loose conjure incenses like Uncrossing, Tranquility, or House Blessing.
- **Physical Exertion Adds to Magical Power:** Never underestimate the sheer power of elbow grease as you sweep, scrub, and mop.
- **Pray While You Work:** Psalms 23 and the Lord's Prayer are well-suited to recite over freshly made scrub water or while cleaning.
- **Use Your Broom in a Magically Significant Way:** Use your broom to sweep away bad luck, turn it upside down to send unwanted people away, and set it across the door to protect a room or building.
- **Fix Your Laundry:** A pinch of well-chosen bath crystals or herbal tea can be added to the rinse cycle of a load of wash. Socks and underwear are particularly well-suited to receiving such treatment.

Learn more about how to clean out crossed conditions in these books:
"Hoodoo Spiritual Baths" by Aura Laforest
"Deliverance!" by Khi Armand

CLEANSED AND BLESSED LAUNDRY SOAP

Mix 2 cups Borax, 2 cups Baking Soda, 2 cups Washing Soda, 2 cups Grated Laundry Soap, 1/2 tablespoon Chinese Wash or Uncrossing Oil, and 1/4 teaspoon House Blessing Oil, dispersing the liquids evenly throughout the blend. Store the mixture in a sealed bucket, away from moisture. Use 2 tablespoons of the powder per full load of laundry.

CONJUREMAN ALI'S TRICKY CLEANING METHOD

ConjureMan Ali offers a clever spiritual cleaning trick: "Add condition oils and crystals to the various cleaning products used in your house, pray over them, and then have a house-cleaning day with all the relatives pitching in. They'll go about the mundane act of cleaning without even realizing that they are using spiritual products to spiritually cleanse your house."

CLEAR THE AIR INCENSE BLEND

Combine a packet each of Hindu Grass, Pine Needle Essential, and Cast Off Evil incense powders. Use this after a fight, an unpleasant conversation or when the energy is heavy. Dispose of the ashes in a crossroads.

MISS CAT'S STRONG HOUSE CLEANSING INCENSE

"Mix Cinnamon with Frankincense, Myrrh, Camphor, and Sandalwood to make a very strong incense. Burn this on charcoal every day for fourteen days to purify a home where bad, violent, or evil things have happened. This incense may also be used to spiritually cleanse clothing received from the dead or from unknown parties. It is said to be good for smoking the entire body too, if you have had to deal with evil people."

SWEEP AWAY THE NASTIES FLOOR SPRINKLE

Combine cut up Broom straws, Basil leaves, and Rue. Sprinkle while praying for removal of whatever "nasties" are concerned. Sweep away or vacuum up and dispose of off your property.

BLESSED THISTLE SPRINKLE

Burn a house blessing petition to ash and mix into a packet of Blessing or House Blessing Sachet Powder. Add a teaspoon of Blessed Thistle. As each room is cleaned, place a pinch of the mix in each corner and one in the center of the room. Say a prayer or portion of scripture as this is done.

WOMEN'S YARD AND GARDEN SECRETS

Evidence of rootwork can be found in many yards and gardens. The following activities can have magical significance:

- **Grow Magical and Medical Plants:** Using a reference book such as *Hoodoo Herb and Root Magic* by Catherine Yronwode, select plants that will grow in your bioregion, either outdoors or in pots or window boxes. Some, like Basil or Rose petals, you can harvest and dehydrate. Others you will keep alive all year round, so that their magical influence will foster and support your wishes.
- **Keep Fowl:** Frizzled hens, particularly black ones, protect against conjure, either pecking it up or scratching it up with their feet. A home flock of Chickens will also provide feathers for whisks and eggs that can be used in personal hands-on cleansing spells.
- **Observe Animal Activity for Omens:** Both pets and wild animals provide divinatory information; their activity can be used to ascertain what will occur in the household. A bird flying into the house, if it does not leave soon, may foretell death; a Cricket on the hearth brings luck.
- **Work with Weather Activity:** Perform love and peace work on sunny days, undertake spells for change when the wind is strong or conditions are unsettled, use snow water to quiet things, and collect thunder-and-lightning water during storms to use in works of anger.
- **Garden by the Moon's Signs:** Learn when to plant, when to harvest, and when to destroy plant pests by working with the Moon. You'll need the *Farmer's Almanac* for this, as the dates change every year.
- **Hang Spell-Work in the Trees:** Make a blue bottle tree to keep off spirits or hang a protective blue bottle filled with glass or mirror shards and your own urine from a tree or a bracket on the porch.
- **Bury Spell-Work on the Property:** Four railroad spikes hammered into the ground at the corners of the house will help you keep your home. Nine Devil's Shoe Strings driven into soft ground across the walkway to the door will keep unwanted people off the property.
- **Sprinkle the Path and the Property Line:** Herbs, washes, mineral dusts, and sachet powders can be sprinkled or scrubbed on the steps leading up to a home to protect or draw influences; lay them around the perimeter of the property to protect the home and its inhabitants.

WHERE ROSEMARY GROWS, THE WOMAN RULES

Rosemary is an evergreen Mediterranean plant in the Mint family with leaves so narrow they resemble Pine needles and a form much like a bonsai conifer. Too tender to survive in the coldest parts of the land, it will thrive outdoors in warm regions and in cold climates it can easily be contained in a large pot which is brought onto a closed porch during the Winter. Rosemary is widely used in cooking (it goes well with poultry) and it is kept near the door, so its leaves can be picked fresh year round. Where Rosemary grows, the woman rules the home, and many a bride receives a gift of potted Rosemary to start her married life off on the right foot.

HOW TO GARDEN BY THE MOON'S PHASES AND SIGNS

• Plant annual flowers and vegetables that bear crops above ground during the waxing of the Moon: from New Moon to Full Moon.
• Plant perennial flowers, bulbs, and vegetables that bear root crops during the waning of the Moon, from Full Moon to New Moon.
• Plant vegetable and flower seeds when the Moon is in the fertile signs of Taurus and Capricorn.
• Transplant flower and vegetable seedlings, as well as shrubs and trees, when the Moon is in the fertile signs of Scorpio, Cancer, or Pisces.
• Pull weeds with the Moon in the barren signs of Gemini, Leo, or Virgo.

POTTED PLANTS AS CONTAINER SPELLS

This advice comes to us from the members of AIRR, the Association of Independent Readers and Rootworkers:

"When a candle cannot be burned on a honey jar, due to the need to keep your work private, you can prepare a sweetening spell inside a hollowed-out red Apple or red Onion, place the loaded and prepared Apple or Onion in the bottom of a flower pot, fill the pot with soil, and plant an herb, flower, or fern in the pot. The potted plant is thus a container spell.

"Citrus plants are associated with spiritual cleansing, road opening, and cutting away negative influences, so a prepared spell in the base of a potted citrus by the entrance to a home will act as a powerful guardian and will purify those who enter. Contrariwise, Cayenne Pepper is used to hot foot and send unwanted people away, so a potted plant spell prepared for hot footing a bad neighbour might take the form of a cute ornamental Chili pepper plant in a pot, with a petition contained in the soil, out of sight."

YOU SHALL REIGN WITHIN YOUR HOME

The amount of light in a house, the presence of pets and plants, the colour of the walls, and the type of ornamentation within are a reflection of the people who live there, and thus your home is the impression of you that greets those who step within your space. Rising and shining in a pleasant home affect the mood. Simply changing the orientation of your furniture or buying new rugs can work significant changes on your psyche. Studying the intentional layout of furniture and other elements according to Asian spiritual principles like Feng Shui and Vastu Shastra can provide a starting point for redecoration, as can home decoration magazines.

Your Home is your castle — become its Queen!

HOW TO FIX AND DRESS HAND-MADE GOODS

One great way to personalize a home is to make items for it. Handicrafts may seem old-fashioned, but the things you make by hand give and show time and care to the home, provide a sense of well-being to those who use them, and can be magically fixed and tricked with your commands.

- **Sewing:** Drapes, bedclothes, and tablecloths are easy and quick to make with a machine. Fix the finished pieces by washing or smoking with House Blessing or Peaceful Home products. Sew your spouse's and your hairs into the hems of bedclothes for fidelity and sexual love.
- **Knitting, Crocheting, and Tatting:** Throws, afghans, and lacy table-cloths or runners can made in a magical manner by adding a prayer or wish with every stitch or turn. Wash or smoke the finished pieces with Stay At Home or Dixie Love spiritual supplies.
- **Quilting:** Quilts make beautiful heirloom pieces to pass on. They can be worked on by all members of a family together and they can also incorporate the outgrown clothing of children or the memory-keeping cloth of an ancestor who has passed on. Praying with each stitch and picturing those we love can produce particularly powerful pieces.
- **Embroidery:** Nothing says "Home Sweet Home" quite like an old-fashioned embroidered motto in a simple wooden frame. Spritz your canvas with Peaceful Home before you start, and when the piece is finished, slip a prayer and a family portrait behind the work, where it will never be seen but its message will radiate out into the room.

HOW TO FIX AND DRESS HOME FURNISHINGS

Almost any piece of furniture can be fixed to suit your purposes. As family members come into contact with them, they are being worked on.

- **Place Objects in or Below Pillows:** Hide charms or packets inside pillows to protect or ward off nightmares or induce visions or dreams of happiness, sexual love, or good fortune.
- **Place Objects in, Behind, or Below the Bed:** Bottle spells, lodestones, mojos, petitions, and herbs go between the mattress and box spring, below the bed or behind the headboard for love.
- **Place Items under Rugs and Mats:** Hide herbs or powders to draw money, love, or protection in the four corners of a room or under a rug, mat, or piece of furniture once the room has been cleaned.
- **Altars:** Be it a small shelf in the back of a closet, a spot above the fridge or on a coffee table or even the corner of a dressing table – all can be turned into small or large altars for purposes useful to you.
- **Brooms:** Small natural fiber or twig brooms can be made into attractive wall-pieces for protection.
- **Candles:** If you can't openly fix a magical candle, dress the hollow candlestick instead and burn the candle "naked" at a family meal.
- **Garlic Braid:** Besides being tasty to use in everyday cooking, a braid of garlic hung on the kitchen wall keeps away the evil eye of jealousy.
- **Horseshoe:** When placed above the front door, the horseshoe is a symbol of luck and prosperity for the home.
- **Mirror:** In a foyer or at exterior windows looking outward, mirrors reflect magical attack and jealous gazes back to their senders.
- **Oil Lamps:** Find an antique lamp at a garage sale or online and fix the reservoir with minerals, herbs, and roots for ongoing work.
- **Packets and Pomanders:** Small sewn or tied parcels of home protection herbs, roots and curios, or Orange and Clove pomanders for luck in the home can be disguised as Christmas ornaments.
- **House Plants:** Adding life and greenery to a home, they also improve air quality and can become a source of food, medicine, and spell-work. Edible magic herbs and lucky bamboo are popular choices.
- **Statuary:** Buy religious, inspirational, or lucky statuary with hollow bases, fill them with prayer papers, herbs, or roots, and seal them.

SPIRITUAL HOME PROTECTION

Once you're in a home you love and cherish, you will want to keep it protected from accidents, intruders, and enemies. Protection magic need not be elaborate, and most practitioners only renew it once a year or as needed.

PROTECTIVE FLOOR WASH
This is a variant of the Lucky Mojo Floor Wash Special, made up specifically for home protection. To a bucket of scrub water, add a tablespoon Chinese Wash; a teaspoon each of Blessed Salt, Epsom Salts, and Saltpeter; plus nine drops of any one of these oils: Cast Off Evil, Fiery Wall of Protection, Jinx Killer, Protection, Uncrossing, Run Devil Run, or Van Van. As you mop or scrub, recite Psalms 121: *"I will lift up mine eyes unto the hills, from whence cometh my help...."*

PROTECTIVE PHOTOS AND PICTURES
A particularly pretty and discreet way to deploy protective charms, herbs, and curios is by making a flat paper packet and sandwiching it between a stitched sampler, photo, painting, poster, or mirror and the frame which holds it. Place it near the entrance, where everyone who comes in will have to pass. Rue, Rosemary, and Mint are good choices here, as is the 7-ingredient Protection Herbs Mixture from Lucky Mojo.

PROTECTION ON THE PATHS OF APPROACH
To deploy protection along the footpath to the home, mix Fear Not To Walk Over Evil or Jinx Killer Sachet Powders with dirt to hide their colour, or simply mix salt and black pepper for the same purpose. A series of nine Devil's Shoe Strings can be buried in a location over which visitors will have to walk, ensuring that if their intention is ill, they'll be tripped up. Sprinkle Red Brick Dust across the doorway.

HIDDEN PROTECTION IN AND AROUND THE HOME
If home repairs are being made, you can hide protective packets or talismans in the walls, above door-jambs, or under newly-laid thresholds. Many people shove a protective charm up the fireplace chimney, or hide it in the basement where it cannot be seen. Packets made for each room may take into account its occupants and uses.

HOME AND FAMILY PROTECTION PACKET

Light some Fiery Wall of Protection Incense in a fireproof bowl, and as it smoulders, write a petition for your safety and that of your family. Turn it clockwise 90 degrees, then cover and cross it with Isaiah 41:10: *"Fear thou not; for I am with thee: be not dismayed; for I am thy God: I will strengthen thee; yea, I will help thee; yea, I will uphold thee with the right hand of my righteousness."* Five-spot the paper with Fiery Wall of Protection Oil and burn it to ash in a fire-proof container.

Lay a square of flannel on a metal plate. In the middle of it place a print of the Solomonic Seal called the Fourth Pentacle of the Moon that has been dressed with the same oil. Put a slice of Solomon's Seal Root and a pinch of White or Yellow Mustard seed on the seal and over this lay the personal concerns of your family members and the petition paper ash. Dress nine Devil's Shoe Strings with the oil and tie them together, wrapping with nine knots and lay it over the other items. Place a small cross charm on the flannel, but not as a part of the packet.

Inscribe your name "and family" in a circle around the wick of each of five white tea lights. Around that carve, *"Fear thou not; for I am with thee."* Dress the lights with the oil. Place four of the candles in a cross around the plate. Place the fifth directly on the herbs and pentacle. While the candles burn, pray your petition and Isaiah 41:10 at least five times. Once the lights have burned, recycle the tins and set the cross to one side.

Fold the flannel toward you, turning clockwise 90 degrees between each fold. When you have a small packet, wrap it tightly with string, always wrapping toward you. Thread the cross onto the string and tie it off with nine knots. Feed the packet with Fiery Wall of Protection Oil. The finished packet can be deployed as desired. That is, it can be kept directly on your person or hidden among your personal effects for protection.

SPIRITUAL PROTECTION WHILE YOU SLEEP

Khi Armand, the author of *Deliverance!*, shares his way to keep a home spiritually safe: "To protect against spirit intrusions and spiritual attacks during the night, keep a Bible open to Psalms 91 under your bed with a pair of open metal scissors laid over the pages. You may anoint the scissors with a protection oil. A Bible once owned by a beloved family member is said to hold power and would be appropriate in such a working. To keep it clean, cover it with clear plastic or, more traditionally, a white cloth."

SETTLING IN WITH THE IN-LAWS

One of the most discouraging moments in a marriage occurs when a wife's in-law family will not respect her. Often it's the mother-in-law who starts the mess, not wanting to accept that her "baby boy" has a new queen in his life. Sometimes it's a jealous, critical sister-in-law who gets the badness going because she wants her "little brother" back under her thumb. In-laws like this are not only ugly guests, they can cause fights between you and your husband — and you may keep on fighting after they have gone home. Here are some ways to put a stop to all the drama:

SWEETEN THEM ALL

Yes, sweeten them all, even the most ignorant, disrespectful, and nasty ones in the lot. They are your husband's people. Don't make him choose, just make them nicer. Half-fill a glass jar with sugar. Write each one's name on a slip of paper, like so: *"God bless [Name], the [relationship] of my husband [Name]. May [she or he] love me as [she or he] loves him, in Jesus' name. Amen."* Don't stop until you name them all, babies, parents, sisters, brothers, cousins, and the family dog. Add sugar as you go, but leave enough air in the jar to shake it. When they come around, shake the jar and use the sugar in the food you serve to them. Replenish the sugar as needed.

HOME-MADE TRIPLE-STRENGTH PEACE WATER

"Before you use commercial Peace Water to bring harmony to your marriage and put a stop to arguments or fights, place Sumac leaves or berries in the bottle and let the bottle stand open under your bed as you make love with your spouse. Afterward, put a little of your mixed sexual fluids in the bottle and shake it up. This 'fixed' Peace Water should be sprayed around the house the same day you fix it, and it will be much, much stronger in power than un-prepared Peace Water, of course." So says Miss cat.

PUT AN END TO QUARRELS IN THE KITCHEN

Deacon Millett, a happily married man, swears by this trick: "If you and your mate always seem to be fussing in the kitchen while meals are being prepared, it may be that the room itself has a jinx on it. A traditional remedy for this is to sprinkle dried Basil on the floor and sweep it out the back door, because 'Evil cannot stay where Basil has been.'"

RETAINING THE SEXUAL SPARK IN MARRIAGE

Romance, passion, sexual frequency, and sexual satisfaction go through ebb and flow in most long term relationships. When romance is fresh, the sex drive is often at its highest. After a few years, routines may set in as partners become habituated with one another and also learn how best to please one another. As relationships mature, issues of children, health, workload, and living situation can change, and these changes may have an impact on sex drive and opportunities for intimacy. None of this need be a problem if we have no specific expectations — but most of us do have preferences, and we often seek to keep our spouses in tune with our needs.

There is no "right" way to engage in sex. If your relationship is good, there's no problem, but unwanted changes should be addressed in the mundane world as well as with magic. A medical doctor or qualified sex therapist may also be of help as you undertake sex-enhancing rootwork.

HERBS, ROOTS, AND CURIOS FOR SEXUALITY
• **Coon Dong (Raccoon Penis Bone):** For virility in men, to keep it hard.
• **Cinnamon:** To heat and spice up love.
• **Cloves:** For loving partnership and friendship as well.
• **Coriander:** To stimulate passion and keep your lover faithful.
• **Damiana:** A reputed aphrodisiac; steep it in wine, strain, and drink.
• **Ginger:** For heat and passion and to warm the fires at home.
• **John the Conqueror Root:** To keep a man virile and sexually strong.
• **Juniper Berries:** For increased male virility and female sensuality.
• **Queen Elizabeth Root:** To attract and hold the love of a man.
• **Sampson Snake Root:** To strengthen men in mind, body, and nature.
• **Sang (Ginseng) Root:** A powerful curio for men's sex and health.
• **Sexual Fluids:** A natural attractant; use in food or as a perfume.

SPIRITUAL SUPPLIES FOR SEXUALITY
• **Adam and Eve:** For natural matedness and procreative sexuality.
• **Fire of Love:** For kindling intimate life and sexual interest.
• **Kiss Me Now!:** For quick sex on short notice.
• **Lucky Clover Vulva Oil:** A feminine lubricant and massage oil.
• **Lucky Swastika Penis Oil:** A male lubricant and massage oil.
• **Nature:** For male health, virility, energy, and sexual prowess.

NATURAL FIDELITY AND TYING HIS NATURE

Many women turn to magic for reconciliation after their marriage has fallen apart, yet experience shows that if you bring back someone who has cheated, the past may be forgiven, but it's seldom forgotten.

On the other hand, if you keep the one you love from going astray, and if you stay faithful as well, your marriage is more likely to last. Here are some old-time conjure spells for fidelity within marriage; they range from gently loving natural fidelity to tying your partner's nature:

HERBS USED FOR NATURAL FIDELITY
• **Balm of Gilead Buds:** A pair of these symbolizes peaceful fidelity.
• **Cumin Seeds:** To keep a lover faithful; can be used in cooking.
• **Dixie John Root:** For a contented stay-at-home marriage.
• **Lodestones:** A matched pair keeps your attraction and bond strong.
• **Lovage Root:** As the name implies, it increases love.
• **Magnolia Leaves:** To ensure fidelity and keep a partner in the home.
• **Periwinkle:** The leaves grow in pairs, symbolizing conjugal fidelity.

DIXIE JOHN ROOT IN THE LAUNDRY
Laundering bedsheets and nightwear with a whole Dixie John Root in a muslin bag keeps the sex-life fresh. It can also be kept on a love altar, below the mattress, or in a mojo bag or bottle spell.

A HEN'S EGG AND A HANDKERCHIEF FOR FIDELITY
Wipe a fresh-laid Hen's egg with a brand-new handkerchief, then wipe your mate's genitals with the handkerchief. Hide the handkerchief in his pillow and he will not stray or wander. Renew the work regularly.

PAY ATTENTION TO YOUR MAN'S SHOES
When your man takes off his shoes, don't let the toes point away from the bed. Keep them neatly toe-in under the bed to keep him coming home.

BURY HIS WASH CLOTH TO KEEP HIM AT HOME
In 1939 a worker in Fayetteville, North Carolina, told Rev. Hyatt how to prevent a man from wandering: Get the cloth with which he washed his genitals and bury it under the eaves of the roof, and it will keep him at home.

MISS CAT'S BED HERBS FOR A FAITHFUL MARRIAGE

"Bed herbs are flat packets sewn inside the mattress for fidelity. They may contain three, seven, or nine of the following herbs: Rosemary, a pair of Balm of Gilead buds, an Angelica Root, Lavender, Rose petals, Coriander seed, Cumin seed, Periwinkle, Chickweed, or whole Magnolia leaves. Additionally, you may sprinkle Cumin seeds under the bed and burn blue candles dressed with Stay With Me Oil so that your mate will remain true."

HOW TO ROOT YOUR MAN TO STAY AT HOME

In 1939, a worker in Wilson, North Carolina, told Rev. Hyatt how to root a man: "Take the dirt out of his foot-track, put it in a cloth and add Salt, Red Pepper, and either Sampson Snake Root or Black Snake Root. Wrap it up, put it in a bottle, stop it up air tight, and bury it. That'll make him stay."

TIE HIS NATURE WITH HIS SOCKS OR UNDERWEAR

Tie his sock to your stocking or pantyhose and bury the pair of them in the back yard, or tie a knot in his drawers and bury that the same way.

TIE HIS NATURE WITH A KNOTTED STRING

Smear his semen on a string cut to the measure of his erect penis. Tie nine knots in the string, one by one. With each knot, call his name, and as he answers, pull the knot tight. He won't be able to get hard with other women.

TIE HIS NATURE WITH A KNOTTED HANDKERCHIEF

To tie a man and make him love you lightly, wipe his semen on a handkerchief and tie one knot in each of its corners, loosely. If you want to make him love you hard, tie the four knots hard and tight. Either way, keep the handkerchief where he will never find it.

TIE HIS NATURE WITH HIS GLOVE-FINGER

In 1939, a root doctor in Florence, South Carolina, told Rev. Hyatt to measure the length of the first joint of the lover's dog finger — the left index finger — and cut nine pieces of broom straw out of your broom to that length, Then obtain your lover's left glove, cut the dog finger part of the glove off, stuff the nine straws into the glove-finger and add nine sewing pins. Tie the bottom of the glove-finer closed and wear it in your pocket, and the person will be tied, will love you, and will not go with another.

MEMPHIS WOMEN GETTING MONEY FROM MEN

On October 30, 1939, these four spells were taught to Rev. Hyatt by four different women in Memphis, Tennessee. Memphis women sure know how to manage their men! The silver dimes that they describe have been replaced with bi-metal coinage, but these tricks should work with any dime.

HIS SILVER DIME, TWO NEEDLES, AND ANISE OIL
"If you want him to give you his money, ask him for money. If he hands you a silver dime, don't you spend that dime. You wrap it in woollen cloth with two needles, a short one and a long one, and you make a wish for to rule him and for to have him bring you that money. And you get you some Anise Oil and keep it anointed with oil and put it in the bottom of your trunk and he'll bring his money to you."

HIS SILVER DIME AND SUGAR SET IN THE CORNER
"You get a silver dime from him and you take that dime and put it in a glass and put two teaspoonfuls of sugar on that dime and set it back in a corner. If he makes any money, he'll bring it to you."

HIS SILVER DIME THAT YOU CARRY "DOWN THERE"
"If a woman has a friend or something and he is able to give her, and can give her money, and it looks like he doesn't and just wants to use her for his convenience, she can get a dime from him and she can take that dime and put it in a brand new piece of domestic (unbleached muslin fabric) and fold it and sew it and wear it next to her and that's good. That'll help out a whole lot in peace with him and he'll provide for her better. Yeah, just pin it right inside her clothes on the right side; wear that down there, next to the skin."

YOUR OWN COINS IN A BAG MADE OF HIS UNDERWEAR
An older woman who kept a brothel and was a professional root doctor did not need to use a man's dime. She said to get a pair of your husband's used underwear and cut the seat out of it. Dress the cloth with Jockey Club Perfume and let it dry, then sew a small bag out of it. Put your own money in this bag and wear it around your waist, beneath your clothes, and tied with a cord so it sits close to your vulva. As long as you wear this you will be able to take advantage of your man, and he will think more of you.

ꝹHE ꝳOTHER

CATCHING A BABY

Not every woman wants to be a mother, and even those who do aspire to motherhood, as well as those who have been blessed with children, may not wish to create life at every fertile cycle or to bring every pregnancy to term. It is your right as a woman to have the children you want, when you want them, with your mate of choice. Many women have fought for your ability to exercise these reproductive rights. Do not give them up lightly.

Prior to planned conception or adoption, it's worth considering what motivates the desire for bringing a new life into the world. If having a child stems from an effort to save a relationship or tie down a partner, you ought to know that it won't accomplish either. If, on the contrary, both partners long for parenthood and are ready to make the commitment, then all that remains is for Nature to smile upon the venture.

The transition from maidenhood to motherhood is physical, as nurturant hormones flood the body, hips widen, and breasts swell. The movement is also psychological, a shift from being responsible solely for yourself to providing for another being. Motherhood changes you in a profoundly spiritual way as well, as you come to know what real compassion, altruism, and unconditional love are. Your young open up a tender spot in your heart that can connect you to goodwill, to softness, and to the human potential for beauty, bringing out the best there is in you.

Simultaneously, children put a mirror to your face and show who you are in the face of adversity, when you're exhausted, overwhelmed, irritated and still on duty. And then there's the worry. Few are the parents I know who can truly sleep without worry or care. Even once the fledgling young have flown the nest, most mothers remain with heartstrings permanently tied to the little ones they let loose.

FERTILITY AMULET
String a munachi charm (LuckyMojo.com/munachi.html), and an evil eye bead (LuckyMojo.com/evileye.html) on a cord. Smoke the amulet in Van Van and Blessing Incense, then oil it with Van Van and Blessing oils. Either wear it or keep it under the conjugal mattress until conception occurs.

DREAMS THAT FORETELL PREGNANCY

If you dream of a fish, you will soon be pregnant. If you dream of a kitten, you will soon be a mother.

BORROWING A BABY

To catch a baby, ask a new mother whose baby is over 40 days old but under 4 months, if you can "borrow the baby." You don't actually take the baby anywhere; instead, you let her nurse it to sleep, hand it to you, and leave the room. Then you lift your blouse and remove the baby's clothes, and quietly cuddle the infant against your naked bosom while it sleeps. You don't attempt to nurse it, just cuddle it, kiss its head, and ask it, while it is sleeping, to go back to Heaven for a minute and fetch you a baby of your own. Then dress the baby, rearrange your own clothes, call the mother back in and return the baby to her.

CONCEPTION MORNING MEAL

Five mornings out of every seven, breakfast on hot oatmeal to which you have added a tablespoon each of ground Flax and honey, plus one of the following: a chopped Apple, five chopped Dates, or three chopped Figs.

A CANDLE SPELL FOR CONCEPTION AND BLESSING

On a Monday during the Waxing Moon, name a white naked female figural candle for yourself. Stick one your own hairs on the head of the candle with warmed beeswax. Soften a lump of beeswax and stick it to the belly of the figure, sculpting a baby bump onto her and making her look pregnant. Anoint the candle with Blessing Oil and dust it with powdered herbs sacred to motherhood and health, such as Motherwort, Angelica, and Flax seed. Light the candle and pray Psalms 102 and 103. Burn the candle straight through. Bury the leftover wax in your front garden or in a potted plant. Repeat monthly until conception occurs.

If your partner wishes to participate, name a white naked male figural candle for him, fix it with his hair, dress it with Blessing Oil and dust it with powdered Calamus, John the Conqueror, and Mullein.

A POCKET PIECE FOR PREGNANCY

Keep a whole Angelica Root as a pocket piece throughout the pregnancy and during delivery. Oil it with Blessing Oil as needed.

AFTERBIRTH CONCERNS

THE PLACENTA

The placenta or afterbirth is a large meaty organ that serves to support the child in the womb. It is ejected from the body soon after the baby has been delivered. Most mammals, as well as members of some human cultures, eat the placenta, as it is a rich source of nourishment and hormones for the new mother, and disposal of it also eliminates a scent that may lead predators to the newborn. Although many people prefer to treat the placenta as medical waste, in Traditional Chinese Medicine, it is valued as a restorative skin rejuvenator. Likewise, a number of popular moisturizing hair conditioners and shampoos marketed in the African-American community contain placenta extracts from Sheep to repair damage and give softness, curl definition, bounce, and shine to the hair.

THE CAUL OR VEIL

The caul, also called the veil, is a portion of the amniotic sac which breaks away during delivery and may remain over the face of the child. If not removed quickly, it can pose a suffocation hazard to the newborn infant. In many countries of the world, special significance is associated to either the caul, those born with one, or both. In conjure, a child born with a veil is seen as gifted with second sight, clairvoyance, the ability to prophesy, and a predisposition to rootwork. The islanders of South Carolina may brew a tea from the caul and give it to the child born with it to keep the child from seeing spirits or being haunted as a result of the gift. Around the world, the caul is often dried and saved as a valuable personal concern. The British, for instance, believe that it preserves against drowning at sea.

THE UMBILICAL CORD

The umbilical cord is quite literally the conduit of the life-blood which nourishes the unborn child. It's a symbol of the link which binds mother and child. Once the stump of umbilical cord that the newborn carries at birth dries and falls off, it can be kept as a potent personal concern in order to work on the child. The jobs most usually performed with it include making mojos to bless the child, spells to protect the child from the rootwork of other women (this is typically performed for sons rather than daughters), and spells to keep the child obedient.

HELP FOR MOTHERS

Having a child entails coming to accept that your life has changed. For every woman who feels that motherhood is the destiny for which she was born, there is another woman struggling to accept her new responsibilities and the loss of her girlish freedom. Women who have supportive mates are more likely to enjoy motherhood. If your man embraces fatherhood, things will go even more smoothly, as two parents make for a lighter load.

The greatest problems besetting new mothers are mundane. They are generally a lack of sleep and difficulty at the outset of nursing.

When it comes to sleep, if a family member is not available to lend a hand, and if you can afford it, consider hiring a post-partum doula to help with housecleaning and cooking. This may allow you to catch a nap now and then until you and the baby settle into a steady routine.

If you have trouble nursing, seek out the free help offered by La Leche League. Since 1956, this nonprofit group has been staffed by volunteers who have breastfed their own babies and are trained to help mothers with breastfeeding. They are available via telephone, Facebook, and Skype.

HERBS FOR INCREASING BREAST MILK
- **Beer:** To help increase the quality and flow of breast milk, stout is suggested. Use it until milk production is stable and then discontinue.
- **Blessed Thistle:** Well reputed to aid in milk production, it's very bitter when brewed into tea. Try capsules.
- **Brewer's Yeast:** This nutritional supplement can be added to cookies and cakes or mixed into smoothies.
- **Fennel:** Eaten as a food or taken as tea, Fennel not only increases milk, but also helps ease colic and improve digestion in the infant.
- **Fenugreek Seed:** Sprinkle the ground-up seeds onto cereal or mix and eat with molasses. Ingesting Fenugreek gives your sweat a sweet, maple-like scent. Don't use it during pregnancy; only after birth.
- **Milk Thistle Seed:** Tea is ineffective in this case, so use the ground whole seed, sprinkled onto cereal or mixed with molasses and eaten.
- **Molasses:** This natural cane-based sweetener is filled with iron and trace minerals which help restore a woman after birth.
- **Oat Flakes:** This humble breakfast cereal is a tonic for the nervous system and a nutritive which helps build the body — and the breast!

HERBAL MAGIC FOR NEW MOTHERS

- **Angelica:** Also called Angel Root and Holy Ghost Root, Angelica helps calm and ground the mind and connect to the inner wellspring of patience and compassion, while protecting the family overall.
- **Blood Root:** One Native American name for this root is Puccoon, and a pair of them, sometimes called a He-Coon and a She-Coon, bond parents together so that they can cooperatively raise their children.
- **Borage:** Reputed to help gladden and uplift the mind and heart. Improves family relationships and communication.
- **Flax:** Used both magically and herbally for the health of children.
- **Lavender:** For greater cooperation and smoother relations, to ease tension, increase fidelity and improve a flagging sex life.
- **Mint:** Cooling and protective, provides mental strength and clarity.
- **Motherwort:** Brings out the maternal and mothering instinct, and helps with mother-infant bonding.
- **Rosemary:** Provides strength and authority to women.

SPIRITUAL SUPPLIES FOR NEW MOTHERS

- **Blessing:** Used for baths and to clean the nursery room.
- **Guardian Angel:** For the safety of children, especially as they enter school or start to travel away from the home.
- **Holy Family:** Symbolic of Catholic family, these supplies are used in conjunction with prayer to help restore peace and happiness within the home. They blend well with Blood Root, Flax, and Angelica.
- **King Solomon Wisdom:** For wisdom in decision-making amidst events of everyday life. Helps resolve custody or child support issues, and encourages compassion on the part of legal or child care services.
- **Our Lady of Grace and Our Lady of the Sacred Heart:** The Catholic Mother can help women find their place of quiet strength, softness and peace even in the hardest of circumstances.
- **Peaceful Home:** For a well-fed, financially stable, happy family without fusses or fights.
- **Protection:** A strong male angel protecting two children is the emblem of fatherhood. Use it to encourage the best from your man, or to ask for help from Heaven if there is no father in the home.
- **Tranquility:** When a new addition to the house limits tranquil moments, this formula helps foster a quiet space in mind and body.

DIRT DAUBER WASP NEST ON THE NAVEL

Mix the fine dirt from a Mud Dauber's nest with Holy Oil or blessed Olive Oil to make a paste. Use the paste to draw an X on the navel of a baby so it will have an "innie" instead of an "outie." This paste can also be used to draw a soothing X on insect bites.

BLOOD ROOT PACKET FOR PARENT-CHILD BONDING

Match a pair of He and She roots and add a smaller root for each child. Fold the roots into a small square of red flannel and bind it tightly with sewing thread. This causes parents to work together for the good of the children and the children to show respect to the parents. Creating a "blood bond" of this type is also useful with foster and adoptive children.

ANGELICA ROOT AND HOLY OIL UNDER THE CRIB

A whole Angel Root tied with a piece of red thread and oiled with 7-11 Holy Oil can be kept in the pocket or worn as a pendant for angelic help in times of stress. Such a root, or a small piece of it, dressed with Guardian Angel or Protection Oil, can be hidden beneath the baby's bed to align the child with heavenly helpers and messengers.

SWEET JAR TO DRAW A FAMILY CLOSER

Prepare a paper on which the name of each person in the family is written. The names should overlap and form a geometric shape. For instance, three names would form a triangle, four a square, and so forth. Encircle the crossed names with an unbroken chain of the words "lovejoyrespect" written repeatedly. Fold a Balm of Gilead bud and a piece of Blood Root for each family member into the paper to form a packet.

Then into a small glass jar filled with honey or syrup, place the prepared petition packet, a pinch of Motherwort, a sprig of Rosemary, a pinch of Borage, a pinch of Deer's Tongue, pinch of Althæa, pinch of Frankincense, and a slice of Solomon's Seal Root.

As you fit the items into the jar, remove some with your finger or a spoon. Eat the honey, speaking aloud between bites, "As this honey is sweet to me, so are we all sweet with each other." Every Sunday or Monday, more often when there's family friction, burn a white or pink candle on the jar. The candles can be dressed with Peaceful Home Oil, Dixie Root in Oil or Blessing Oil.

TO PROTECT CHILDREN FROM BAD DREAMS

If your children have trouble sleeping or are afraid of nightmares, wash them head-to-toe in Chamomile tea and give them Chamomile tea to drink. Put their photos in a Bible at Psalms 121 and keep the Bible in their room.

MISS PHOENIX'S PROTECTION FOR KIDS IN SCHOOL

"This spell is to support the safety of children in school, and to do so discreetly. You will need a small square of fabric and some thread the same colour as your child's backpack. Write out the child's name in list form seven times and encircle the name with your petition. Be specific and use words like "protection, security, safety." Anoint a Cat's Eye shell with Protection Oil as you call on your ancestors to guide and protect their descendant. Place the Cat's Eye shell, an a pinch each of Salt, Basil, and Rosemary on the paper and fold it over towards you. Rotate the paper one tine clockwise and fold it towards you again. Repeat the pattern one more time.

"Dip your thread in Protection Oil and sew the petition paper into the backpack using the square of fabric as a pouch. This will keep it hidden from anyone looking, including your child!

"It is good to refresh this working at least once a week by anointing the hidden pouch with Protection Oil, restating your prayers and calling on your ancestors for their guidance and protection each time. A new pouch should be made for each school year."

DRESS CHILDREN'S HAIR WITH SPIRITUAL SUPPLIES

As you comb, brush, pin up, braid, or fix your children's hair, you have the perfect opportunity to introduce some magic into their lives. Crown of Success Oil is especially appropriate for dressing the head. Add it to conditioners or lightly smooth it in by hand as you fix their hair.

DON'T LET YOUR CHILDREN BOTHER BIRDS' NESTS

In 1939 in Waycross, Georgia, a wise old male root doctor, whom Rev. Hyatt called "Dr. Heard," commanded that men must not let their wives or children "run about in the woods and disturb the birds in their nests as they are laying eggs." If they do, he said, "Trouble will grow in your family." He also noted that Bluebirds can poison those who rob their nests. "Whatever you do, remember, don't let your children ramble in the forest and bother those little fowls while they are laying their eggs in their nests!"

ᎢHE GRANDMOTHER

Grandmotherhood is neither sought by, nor granted to, every woman, and for those who become grandmothers, emotions and circumstances range widely. At its most ideal, grandmotherhood is a happy blend of shared care and meaningful special moments with sweet children, but some grandmothers are sadly cast out of their grandchildren's lives, while others are unfairly forced to shoulder the duties of late-life childcare due the inability of their children to rear their own children.

If your grandchildren live in the home with you, the spells you perform on their behalf, such as protection and giving them an advantage in school, can be worked through bathing, hair dressing, and laundering their clothes with spiritual supplies, just as a mother would. These home-style spells can also be done when visiting, or when the grandchildren visit you.

Another typical form of grandmother work is the giving of tricked or fixed gifts, things the child will treasure and keep.

A SIMPLE PHOTO IN A FRAME

Get a photo made of you and the grandchild at a happy moment in a recognizable place that has a chance of enduring for decades. Do not take the photo in a portrait studio or in your living room; rather, stand beside a historic monument or a great piece of architecture. There should be no one in the photo but the two of you. If you have multiple grandchildren, make one for each child. Place a small print of the picture in an elegant frame. Hand write a little note with your names, the date, and the place, and slip it in the frame behind the photo. Give the framed photo to the child and say, "Now, whenever you pass by [the place], you'll remember me and the fun day we had there." The child will be imprinted on that memory, and will always think of you when walking or driving past that place.

WHEN ROCKS ARE BETTER THAN SOCKS

It is nice to give children clothes, and of course you can pre-launder such gifts in Blessing Bath Crystals, but children outgrow their clothes quickly. A magical teddy bear or a collection of rock crystals, sea shells, or old coins, also prepared and fixed, is never outgrown, and many people keep that old bear or that old rock, coin, or shell collection from Granny all their lives.

THE WIDOW

Not every woman marries and not every married woman outlives her mate and becomes a widow. However, statistically speaking, most women who marry are partnered with men, and most women live longer than most men by about seven years. Therefore widowhood is the lot of many woman.

Despite how common it is, widowhood is not a state of life celebrated or revered by our society. It is generally portrayed as lonely, and, truth to tell, for many women it is. For this reason some widows seek remarriage, and fall in love again. Even older women may find love to be a great blessing in the latter half of life — and a post-menopausal woman in love is not much different than a young one. In fact, she may employ all of the same tricks of conjure she used when young, merely substituting vaginal fluid or a drop of urine for menstrual blood if she once worked that way.

On the other hand, if a widow is content to communicate in spirit with her mate who has gone on before, she may choose permanent widowhood. In a case like this, the departed spouse may remain with her in spirit form.

A WIDOW'S LOCKET

One of the most potent remembrances of a person is a photo. Another deeply symbolic memento is a lock of hair. In Victorian times, both of these tokens were used, singly and in combination, to create memorial jewelry and mourning art that commemorated the beloved dead. To revive this tradition, all you need is a hinged locket with two spaces under glass to enclose a photo and a lock of hair. Elaborate hair ornaments and brooches can be plaited, braided, or macraméd of hair. Large works of hair art are not worn, but are framed under glass and hung on the wall.

A HOME SHRINE TO A DEPARTED PARTNER

A sacred memory space or shrine to your beloved can be simple or elaborate, as you prefer. Start with a framed photo, behind which you have hidden a handwritten letter of love and, if possible, a lock of hair. In a small container, keep your mate's graveyard dirt, or, with the trend toward cremation rather than earth-burial, you may choose an urn of cremains instead. Add flowers. Changing them regularly will strengthen your devotion. Light a candle when you wish to converse with your mate's spirit.

Starting Over

TRY, TRY AGAIN

Almost no one on Earth lives a perfectly linear life, like a grand cruise ship sailing through the Panama Canal. In our lives there are often many setbacks — the end of an affair, a break-up just before marriage, a miscarriage, the death of a loved one, the need to relocate, a divorce, or more. In the wake of these alterations to our hopes and plans, we may experience confusion, sorrow, and a loss of purpose. After the grief recedes, which may be a time measured in years, not months, we have the opportunity to start again. The path may be different, but we are still alive, still ready for happiness, and still able to help ourselves with magic.

In this chapter several forms of "starting over" are described, with conjure spells appropriate to each, to help return you to your chosen path:

OPENING YOURSELF TO CHANGE

Coming to terms with uncertainty during the in-between periods when jobs, partners, children, friends, family, and self are in flux, requires a masterful balance of strength, fluidity, and faith. It may seem that you're just hanging on or just about to fall apart — yet that recognition itself is a sign of courage. Although difficult for pretty much everyone, these are times of reassessment, as different avenues open up and offer new vistas.

We needn't remained fixed tableaus at any time in our lives. The words and values we choose to define ourselves can change with the years. Our actions can take bold new directions if we permit it. No matter how stagnant things have become, fostering personal power can help thin the mud keeping our feet stuck in place.

Magic offers us a unique way to show our faith in the future while guiding the direction that change takes; it creates structure in the chaos and brings shape to the fluidity. When dealing with a massive life change, I like to prepare the way by working complex spells which involve the physical movement of items like candles and the elaborate deployment of spell remains; the greater the changes, the more intense the spell.

SPELL FOR TRANSITION AND TIMES OF CHANGE

Mix King Solomon Wisdom, Clarity, and Tranquility Bath Crystals in a glass jar. Mix Clarity and Tranquility Incense in another jar. Grind Yarrow, Solomon's Seal Root, and Sampson Snake Root to powder as you pray for calm, wisdom, and guidance through your time of transition, and set aside. Get up before dawn and bathe with 1/5 of the bath crystals in the water. Wash upward from feet to face and fingertip to shoulder. Air dry, dress in clean clothes, and sprinkle a sample of the bath water up your front steps, toward the door. Next, set up an altar on a metal cookie sheet. Burn the incense mix while you work. Write your name on a paper nine times, fold it toward you, add in a couple of your hairs, tape it to the glass of a zodiacal vigil light of your own sign, and set it in the center of the space. Place a printed or hand-drawn copy of the 7th Pentacle of the Sun from *The Key of Solomon* under it. This is you. With King Solomon Wisdom Sachet Powder draw a triangle around the candle, point upward, leaving space for three roots. Draw a powder circle around the triangle, touching it at its tips.

Fix a white vigil light with the herbs, plus Clarity, Tranquility, and King Solomon Wisdom oils. Pray for peace and protection, repeating, "I am safe and protected." Set the candle at the top point of the triangle. Place three Devil's Shoe Strings tied with string and secured with five knots between the candles, saying "Protect me from harm and trip up any adversity."

Fix a blue vigil light with the herbs and oils, praying for peace of mind and tranquility, repeating, "I live with ease." Set the candle at the lower right tip of the triangle. Put a John the Conqueror Root between the candles, saying, "Bring me confidence and ease."

Fix a purple vigil light with the herbs and oils, praying for power and mastery, repeating, "I am confident and act masterfully, flexible in the wind of change." Set the candle at the lower left tip of the triangle. Put a Master Root between the candles, saying "Bring me mastery and power."

The lights will burn about five days. Each day, bathe, light incense, and pray Deuteronomy 31:6 (*"Be strong and of a good courage, fear not, nor be afraid..."*) When the lights are done, put the roots, name paper, Seal of Solomon, and some herb mix in a red bag with an Owl charm. Smoke it in incense, breathe into it Deuteronomy 31:6, tie it, and feed it with the oils. Keep it on you or in your pillow-case. Drop the used sachet powder in a crossroads. Every week, until the transition is complete, dress a 4" white candle with the oils and herbs, light it and some incense, then feed the mojo.

RECONCILIATION, REUNION, AND RENEWAL

If you and your mate have suffered a separation or break up, you should work fast to return, reconcile, reunite, or renew the relationship.

Return means to bring someone back, no matter why the person left. Reconciliation means to settle all quarrels. Reunion means to take up where you left off as a couple. Renewal means to get a fresh start. These are not the same, and there are spells for each of these conditions.

While working for return or reconciliation, maintain contact without being pushy. Don't pressure your ex, simply remind him or her that you're still around and you can both have a good time. Don't worry about what your ex is thinking. It's simply not worth your time or energy at this stage.

As a root doctor, I have noticed a pattern among women who undertake reunion work: What begins as reconciliation mutates into domination, cursing, and "suffer-for-having-hurt-me" spells. Among those who work with spirits, I see a transition from petitioning Mother Mary, to Saint Martha, to Santisima Muerte, to the Intranquil Spirit. I can tell you from experience that this doesn't usually foster reconciliation; instead it pushes it further away. A love song is nice, a love sledgehammer, not so much.

An obsessive desire to bring back an ex is often less driven by love, and more by neediness, by a fear of being alone and by one's self-definition relying on being in a relationship. I'm not saying that this is always the case, nor that more coercive work doesn't have its place — in certain specific circumstances — but it is worth exploring how your self-confidence ties into your romantic affairs as you assess what motivates your hope for reconciliation and how it affects your magical intentions.

If you have a tendency to obsess on the ex or the outcome of your work, I suggest that you hire someone to work on your behalf rather than undertake it solo. Then, excepting any contact work, use your time to take a class in something that interests you, join a social club, enjoy the company of family and friends, and cast a spell to boost your own personal power. The happier and more independent you are, the more likely that a reunion can occur. Take the time to heal so you can be a whole partner.

Finally, as I always tell my clients: Set a time limit on your work. If it is not meant to be, you will still have time left in life to find another love.

For an entire book of spells devoted to reunion with an ex, see: "Hoodoo Return and Reconciliation Spells" by Deacon Millett

INCENSE SPELL FOR THE RETURN OF A PARTNER

Prepare an incense mixture of Dragon's Blood resin, Sandalwood chips, and Myrrh resin, and burn a small amount on charcoal. In the smoldering bed of incense, burn to ash a small paper on which is written your wish for the return of your partner. Repeat daily.

DOLL-BABY TO BRING A PARTNER BACK

Hand-sew a doll-baby from a piece of your ex's worn clothing, sock, or underwear. Dip your sewing thread in a mix of Reconciliation and Return To Me oil and use only back-stitches. At each stitch, say aloud, "Come back." Stuff the dollie with your ex's personal concerns, photo, or name paper; a piece of Calamus Root and a few Poppy petals at the head; a small John the Conqueror Root and two Balm of Gilead buds at the heart; and a mix of Rose petals, Periwinkle, Lavender, Master of the Woods, Forget-Me-Not, Spanish Moss, and Thistle fluff for the rest of the body.

Baptize the doll in the name of your ex and talk sweet to it at least once a week, or daily if you can. Tell the doll how things will be once you reconcile; how you'll love each other, care for each other, and respect each other. Rub the doll on your body, and then smoke it in Tobacco incense to carry the words to your lover's mind. Keep the doll in your bed or tied inside a pair of your sexiest underwear, when you aren't working it. Make sure the work stays hidden from prying eyes.

DOCTOR ENGLISH TELLS HOW TO REUNITE A COUPLE

In 1937 in Norfolk, Virginia, Rev. Hyatt interviewed Doctor English, a professional hoodoo man with 35 years of experience in the work. Born in Chicago, Illinois, English was widely travelled and knew hundreds of old spells, for he collected them himself. This one is to bring back someone who has left home: "Place the person's name on a lineless piece of white paper and repeat the words, *'In the Name of the Father, Son, and Holy Ghost, John So-and-So may return home. In the Name of the Father, Son, and Holy Ghost, and will be contented when returned.'* Place the name paper under a saucer and put Cinnamon and granulated sugar on the saucer. Pitch the contents of the saucer into his old room for nine mornings at three o'clock in the morning, calling his name and saying, *'Return home in nine day's time.'* That is an old one that was learned to me by Doctor Gorse. He was out in Chicago way for some time."

MOVING CANDLE SPELL TO RETURN YOUR HUSBAND

In February, 1940, as Rev. Harry Hyatt was wrapping up four years of collecting conjure spells from African-American practitioners, he recorded an early example of what we now call a "moving candle spell." In this version each candle stays in one place, but the series of candles inches its way toward the worker. His informant was a woman in Algiers, Louisiana:

"If your loved one is gone, your man or your husband, or whomsoever, and you want him back, you get nine pink altar candles and a sheet of white parchment paper, and write his name nine times on the paper, like a list.

"I tried this myself. What I am telling you, I did that myself. So I know.

"Set the paper on the table with the head of the paper facing you, and set the first candle at the bottom name, farthest from you. And every candle you set, you set it up higher, toward you a little, one name at a time. The first candle you put down at the bottom of the paper on the first name, right there. After you have burned that one, see, you set the next candle at the second name. And each candle is on the next name.

"Now, when you go to light each candle, you wash it. You wash your candle first, but you turn it bottom upward so that the wick won't get wet, and you wash it off only at the bottom with clean water and just let the water drip off it. Then you light that candle.

"And then you get that Temple Incense. That goes with those candles. [Temple Incense was a popular brand at that time; an equivalent brand is Lucky Spirit Incense.] You burn that incense. You put a little dribble of it, say a dram, in a saucer. Then you put the candle in another saucer and you burn that light on the paper. See, each kind of candle has an incense that makes the smoke that goes with the reason for burning that candle.

"Now, sometimes in burning these candles it'll bring your man back before nine days. And he'll come unexpectedly. When he appears at the door, you've got to rush back and pinch it out. Don't blow it out. You'll have to wet your fingers and pinch the light out.

"I burn these candles in a zinc wash tub, because, you know, a candle is something that catches fire sometimes if it falls over. So you put both saucers and the paper in a tub and you burn it in your private room where you sleep. That means in your bedroom, not in your front room, but right in your back bedroom; neither in the side rooms nor the hall. You've got to burn it right where you sleep, in your bedroom, to bring back your loved one. It's got to be right there, where you're at."

HOW TO GET A GOOD DIVORCE

In some cases, the best way to approach a relationship is to leave it. Some situations warrant immediate exit — cases involving violence, drugs or sexual abuse for example. Other situations allow for a more deliberate and planned decision to leave. Neither way is an easy decision to make and both can have repercussions in the emotional, social, and financial spheres.

When possible, divorce is easier to move through if you begin putting money aside ahead of time. Setting up and building a secret fund or private account with about a year's worth of income in it allows for a much softer landing following the choice to endarelationship.

SEPARATION VERSUS BREAK UP

In bringing about a magical parting, the most widely used formulas are Break Up and Separation. They are employed to fix personal items or to anoint figural or plain candles in a moving candle spell.

Miss Cat explains the difference: "Separation spiritual supplies are customarily used when the idea is for a calm, strong path toward disentanglement with no fights, problems, or left-over hard feelings. Some folks think of Separation as a "weaker" form of the famous Break Up product line, but that is incorrect. It is not "weaker;" it is different. It is deliberately made with a measure of healing and calming herbs as well as those that will tend to drive folks apart. Separation products and spells are especially useful when there are issues of child support and child custody involved or when the parties who are breaking up will continue to be employed at the same job site or attend the same school."

A PSALM FOR ABUSED WIVES

If you are being physically, verbally, or sexually abused in your home, get out! Seek help at once. Also, write out this portion of scripture and carry it on you or wear it in your shoe: Psalms 140: *"Keep me, O Lord, from the hands of the wicked; preserve me from the violent man...."*

ANGELIC PROTECTION FROM A THREATENING MAN

If you fear that your soon-to-be-ex's reaction to your leaving may be harmful, angry, or violent, dress a whole Angelica root with Fiery Wall of Protection Oil and carry it in a conjure bag with a Saint Michæl medal.

WAX CANDLE DOLL TO STOP AN ABUSIVE MAN

Baptize a naked figural candle for the man. Heat a knife by candle-flame while you tell the doll, *"You are done causing hurt; your hands can no longer do harm."* Cut the hands from the candle while reciting Psalms 140:4: *"Keep me, O Lord, from the hands of the wicked; preserve me from the violent man; who have purposed to overthrow my goings."* Place the hands in a heavy fire-safe dish. Stand the candle in front of the dish, splash Florida water on the hands and set them alight while the doll watches.

The next day, heat the knife while you tell the doll, *"You can no longer follow me nor move at all."* Cut the feet off the candle while reciting Psalms 140:1: *"Deliver me, O Lord, from the evil man: preserve me from the violent man."* Place the feet in the dish. Stand the candle in front of it, splash Florida water on the feet, and set them alight while the doll watches.

On the third day, if there has been sexual abuse, now is the time to use the hot knife to cut away the wax figure's genital area and burn it while the figure watches. With or without that consideration, light the wick of the candle while reciting Psalms 140:10: *"Let burning coals fall upon [Name]: let [Name] be cast into the fire; into deep pits, that [Name] rise not up again."* After the candle burns out, bury the spell remains in a graveyard.

A similar spell can be worked with a chinaware doll instead of a figural candle. Rather than cutting away the pieces, each day the appropriate member is broken off the doll using a hammer and chisel. On the final day, the entire doll is smashed to bits, with disposal in a graveyard.

BACK TO BACK MOVING CANDLE SPELLS FOR DIVORCE

A simple moving candle for divorce can be worked with two black figural candles, one for each person. Stand them back to back, dress their backs with Separation or Break Up Oil, and walk them slowly away from each other as they burn, either on one day or in sessions over several days.

A FOUR-CANDLE SPELL FOR DIVORCE AND NEW LOVE

Fix a figural candle for each partner, plus one for each of their future unknown lovers. As the separating candles move away from one another, they approach the figures symbolizing new and rewarding relationships. In addition to Separation or Break Up Oil on their backs, they are dressed on their fronts with Attraction or Love Me Oil to bring the unknown lovers in, creating satisfaction and joy for both parties in the divorce.

DEVI SPRING'S PEACEFUL PARTING SPELL

This spell comes from Devi Spring of Queen of Pentacles Conjure: "Separation products are used for a peaceful parting. I consulted on a work for a married couple where one partner wanted to divorce, but the other was really fighting it. I had my client take two figural candles, dress them with Separation Oil, and loosely tie the candles together with one string for each year that they had been married, in this case seven years.

"I had the client dress a pair of scissors with Separation Oil, too, asking the Divine to use it to help both partners cut ties to one another peacefully. Each day, my client would cut one of the ties and burn the candles while praying for a peaceful separation. Once all the strings were cut, the client placed a line of Separation Bath Crystals and the open scissors between the two figures, lit them, and walked them apart a bit each day for seven days.

"During this time, I also had the client dressing the bed sheets with Separation Sachet and diffusing Separation Oil in the house as an air freshener. At the end of the 14-day spell, I told the client to wrap the partner's candle remains in a white cloth with Blessing Powder, pray that the partner find happiness and a blessed life, and throw the bundle into running water to help it carry the partner away, toward a better life.

"In this case, within 6 weeks my client's partner went from fighting tooth and nail and making the situation extremely ugly and contentious, to just peacefully accepting things and moving out without any drama. They have since amicably signed all the legal paperwork separating their lives."

PROTECTION FROM AN EX OR UNWANTED LOVER

To keep an ex from coming around, bury nine Devil's Shoe Strings upright like little soldiers on the walk up to the house or at the threshold. Pray for protection as you bury each root, asking it to *"Keep [Name] from coming around."* Sprinkle Barberry, Knotweed, and Salt across the doorways and windows every week, forming a line to bar the way.

CHILD SUPPORT WITH A DOLLAR AND AN OLD PHOTO

Get a photo of you holding the child, with the father beside you. Cut it apart to cut him from the child. Place a dollar bill behind the pieces, so George Washington's face (the government) both links and separates him and the child, then tape it in place. Dress the money with Pay Me Sachet Powder. This forces him to pay child support to see the child.

ᵀHE ᴴOODOO ᴸADY

One needn't be a professional root doctor or hoodoo woman to work on someone else's behalf. Most women have within them a bit of the witch.

Our mystical female power can be used to support the well-being of those around us as we step in to defend and protect the people we love, or those who can't help themselves. When we work to protect a child or lover from coercive magic, or when we act to free a friend or family member from a difficult predicament, we are hoodoo ladies at work. We become part of the female community that protests and fights for social justice and equality in a world that so often conspires to pull the ground from beneath our feet. We do this in our actions, and we do this spiritually in our magic.

We are also conjure women of a more sorcerous type, when we work to unravel evil. A freezer spell to stop someone from messing up the lives of your family or friends is justified witch work. A retaliatory mirror spell that returns dark or evil spells to those who cast them is also the justified work of a witch. Spiritual revenge against those who harm pets, children, friends, family, or the life of our planet are also justified, and may be pursued even unto death, if God so wills.

The root woman is not a fast gun for hire. She does not serve everyone, and although she may charge for her services, she selects the cases she takes, and she may volunteer as much time in the community as she charges for. Above all, no matter what her age, she is a wise woman, someone whom people come to for advice and healing, and to learn the tricks of conjure.

FREEZER SPELL TO KEEP A RIVAL "ON ICE"

If another woman is flirting with your man, you can put her "on ice." Get her photo and write her name and birth date on it. Next take something of her body, such as a hair, a piece of jewelry, or a loose thread from her clothing, and fold it into her photo. Lay out a piece of aluminum foil, and on top of it place a folded paper towel. Wet the paper towel with water and Red Pepper hot sauce and fold the paper name-packet into it, then fold the aluminum foil around the paper towel, to make a flat packet. Stick this way back in your freezer to chill out the other woman's interest in your man.

PROTECTING YOUR SON FROM BEWITCHING WOMEN

One way for a mother to protect her son is to craft a jar spell containing Salt, Frankincense, Rosemary, Blood Root, and Grains of Paradise, along with the umbilical cord stump of the baby boy. Keep the closed jar hidden in your room; an upper closet shelf is a good place for it. The jar need not be worked with candles or shaken like a vinegar or honey jar, it is simply kept hidden for as long as the protection is required, hiding the son's spirit from women wishing to ensnare him.

SHIELDING YOUR SON WITH YOUR BLOOD

Snip a lock of the baby's hair and tie it with a string dressed with a combination of your menstrual blood and Holy Oil. Place it in an envelope in the family Bible. Your protective blood will cause interference whenever a woman tries to feed your son menstrual blood.

RAW EGGS FOR BREAK UPS AND HOT FOOTING

- **For a break up:** Write the name of one party at one end of the egg and the second party at the other end, not touching. Use a needle to pierce each end and stir up the contents. Bury the egg in an Ants' nest.
- **To move someone away:** Write the person's name all over an egg, every which way. Use a knife point to pierce one end and introduce Red Pepper powder, Black Pepper powder, and Graveyard Dirt into the egg. Take the prepared egg to your enemy's house and throw it over the roof to break it. Throw toward the West if possible.

TO FREE SOMEONE WHO IS CONFUSED IN MIND

Baptize a white skull candle for the person afflicted, hollowing out a little divot underneath, loading it with personal concerns, and sealing it with wax. Wash the candle with Holy Water or Florida Water, being careful to avoid getting water on the wick. Let the candle air dry and anoint it with Clarity Oil. Oil the eye sockets, speaking Psalms 119:18 as a petition: *"Open (Name's) eyes, that (he/she) may behold wonderful things from your law."* Oil the ears, reciting Psalms 119:130, *"The unfolding of your words gives light; It gives understanding to the simple."* Light the candle and let it burn, praying Psalms 119:176, *"(Name) has gone astray like a lost sheep; seek thy servant; for (he/she) does not forget thy commandments."* Dispose of any spell remains in a crossroads.

BLACK WALNUTS TO TAKE OFF A LOVE SPELL

If you are having trouble leaving a relationship because someone put a love spell on you, boil nine Walnuts in three quarts of water until the water reduces to one quart and turns brown. Write your ex's name on a paper, and set it under a very small candle in the bathroom. Light the candle, fill the tub with water, and throw in the boiled Walnuts and brown water. Bathe from head to feet, renouncing your former lover, and when you are done, burn the name-paper in the candle flame. Throw a remnant sample of your leftover bath water into a crossroads or against a tree.

REVERSING SPELL WITH TWO TIED MIRRORS

Catherine Yronwode teaches this simple way to reverse a curse: "Get two small square or round mirrors. Have a photo of the enemy, plus hair, fingernail clippings, or other concerns. Make a small copy of the photo and use it as your petition paper, writing the name and your command on the back. Draw arrows in the four corners of the name-paper, pointing outward. Dress the corners with Reversing Oil, blended with a specific condition oil such as Stop Gossip Oil or Fiery Wall of Protection Oil. In this example, we will add Stop Gossip Oil, and petition accordingly. Place a pinch of Red Pepper in the packet, along with the personal concerns, saying, *"May your lying words burn in your mouth if you ever speak ill of me again!"* Fold the paper away from you, photo side out, turn it counter-clockwise, and fold it again. Set the name-paper in the middle of one mirror and say, *"May all you say about me reflect your evil back to you!"* Place the other mirror on top, facing in, and tie the mirrors together with black thread, as if wrapping a package. Lay the trick where the person will have to walk over it."

MISS AIDA'S DEATH BY DEHYDRATION SPELL

In her book, *Cursing and Crossing,* Miss Aida offers a simple but extremely effective method to make an enemy wither away: "Take a large, fresh, and healthy leaf from any plant or tree. With a fine-point marker (preferably black in colour), write the person's name and birth date on the leaf. Secure the leaf somewhere outside where it will be continuously exposed to the rays of the Sun. As the leaf dehydrates and withers away, so will the person. The remains will resemble ashes when crumbled. Either throw the remains down the sewer, to the crossroads, or scatter them on a pathway near the person's trail."

HERB BATH TO UNTIE YOUR OWN NATURE

If your nature has been tied by a rival who wants to kill your sex drive, here's how to break off the negative work. You will need 3 parts Nettle, 1 part each Sarsaparilla root, Hyssop, and Angelica Root, and 1/2 part Sage. Boil the Angelica and Sarsaparilla while envisioning yourself as the sensual woman you were before being tied. Simmer the roots for 15 minutes, turn off the heat, add the Nettle, Hyssop, and Sage, and steep for half an hour. Add the herb tea to your bath and reserve a cup to dilute and drink. It won't taste great, but it does the job and it's non-toxic. However, do not consume it if you're pregnant, as both Angelica and Hyssop are contra-indicated in pregnancy.

UNBINDING A MAN BOUND BY MENSTRUAL BLOOD

You can cleanse a man who has been bound by the use of menstrual blood at the start of a new relationship, to ensure that things begin with a clean slate, or after a wandering partner has returned and you suspect that conjure may have played a part in his cheating or absence.

- **Baths:** Bathe him with Rue, Nettle, Burdock, Sampson Snake Root, Black Walnut, or 13-Herb Bath, mixed with Uncrossing, Jinx Killer, or Van Van Bath Crystals. Follow the next day with a love bath.
- **Incense:** Thoroughly smoke his entire body in an appropriate blend of loose powder incense such as Uncrossing. He will have to be a willing participant for this however.
- **Teas:** Herb teas that uncross coercive love work include Burdock, Nettle, and Lemon Grass. They can be administered in other drinks.
- **Mercury Dime Decoction:** File the ridges off a silver dime, boil them in milk, let the milk cool, pour it off the filings, and drink it warm. The filings can be dried and saved and used at least two more times.

HOW TO CUT FREE A MAN WHOSE NATURE IS TIED

Instruct the man to buy a brand new folding pocket knife, take it to a river or creek, walk into the water, undo his pants, and unfold the knife, slowly, blade side up, just below waist level. Tell him to urinate in such a way that the knife blade splits the stream of urine to cut the knots that tied him. His urine flow should fall in the water to be swept downstream. When done, he is to slowly fold the knife halfway upward, to restore his ability to get an erection, then snap it shut, fasten his pants, and walk home, holding the knife, and drop it behind him at any crossroads along the way.

BIBLIOGRAPHY

Aida, Miss. *Cursing and Crossing*. Lucky Mojo Curio Co., 2017.

Alexander C. {Claude Alexander Conlin]. *Personal Codes*. MISC, 2011.

Armand, Khi. *Deliverance!* Missionary Independent Spiritual Church, 2015.

Bhutta, Mahmood F. "Sex and the Nose: Human Pheromonal Responses." *J. R. Soc. Med.*, 2007.

Buckley, Sarah J. "Placenta Rituals and Folklore". *Midwifery Today*, Winter, 80:58-9, 2006.

Chireau, Yvonne P. *Black Magic: Religion and the African American Conjuring Tradition.* University of California Press, 2003.

Cunningham, Scott and David Harrington. *The Magical Household*. Llewellyn Publications, 1983.

DeClaremont, Lewis. *Legends of Incense, Herb, and Oil Magic*. Lucky Mojo Curio Co., 2016.

Falcao, Ronnie. "Medicinal Uses of the Placenta". GentleBirth.org/archives/eatplcnt.html Accessed 3/14/17.

Farrar, Janet and Stewart. *Spells and How They Work*. St-Edmundsbury Press, 1990.

Federal Writers' Project. *Slave Narratives: A Folk History of Slavery in the United States From Interviews with Former Slaves*. Library of Congress, 1936-1938.

Gamache, Henri. *The Master Book of Candle Burning*. Original Publications, 1998.

Gardback Johannes Bjorn. *Trolldom*. Y.I.P.P.I.E., 2015.

Gladstar, Rosemary. *Herbal Healing for Women*. Simon and Shuster Inc., 1993.

Gottlieb, Alma and Thomas Buckley. *Blood Magic: The Anthropology of Menstruation*. University of California Press, 1988.

Hyatt, Harry Middleton. *Hoodoo – Conjuration – Witchcraft – Rootwork*. (Five Vols.) Memoirs of the Alma Egan Hyatt Foundation, 1970-1978.

Ladies Auxiliary of Missionary Independent Spiritual Church. *Hoodoo Food!: The Best of the Conjure Cook-Off and Rootwork Recipe Roundup*. Missionary Independent Spiritual Church, 2014.

Laforest, Aura. *Hoodoo Spiritual Baths*. Lucky Mojo Curio Co., 2014.

LeFæ, Phoenix. *Hoodoo Shrines and Altars*. Missionary Independent Spiritual Church, 2015.

Michæle, Miss and Prof. Charles Porterfield. *Hoodoo Bible Magic*. Missionary Independent Spiritual Church, 2014.

Millett, Deacon. *Hoodoo Honey and Sugar Spells*. Lucky Mojo Curio Co., 2013.

Millett, Deacon. *Hoodoo Return and Reconciliation Spells*. Lucky Mojo Curio Co., 2015.

Ott, Jonathan. "Pharmaka, Philtres, and Pheromones". *MAPS*, Volume XII No. 1, Spring 2002.

Porterfield, Charles. *The Sporting Life*. Lucky Mojo Curio Co., 2016.

Puckett, Newbell Niles. Folk Beliefs of the Southern Negro. Univ. of North Carolina Press, 1926.

Riva, Anna. Golden Secrets of Mystic Oils. International Imports, 1990.

Riva, Anna. Magic with Incense and Powders. International Imports, 1985.

Selig, Godfrey A. Secrets of the Psalms. Dorene Publishing Co., 1982.

Young, Sharon M. and Daniel C. Benyshek. "In Search of Human Placentophagy". *Ecology of Food and Nutrition*, 49:6, 467-84, 2010.

Yronwode, Catherine. Hoodoo Herb and Root Magic. Lucky Mojo Curio Co., 2002.

Yronwode, Catherine. Hoodoo Rootwork Correspondence Course. Lucky Mojo Curio Co., 2006.

Yronwode, Catherine. Paper In My Shoe. Lucky Mojo Curio Co., 2015.

Yronwode, Catherine and Mikhail Strabo. The Art of Hoodoo Candle Magic. Missionary Independent Spiritual Church, 2013.

Yronwode, Catherine et al. The Black Folder. Missionary Independent Spiritual Church, 2013.